HONEST

Also by Lucien Young

Alice in Brexitland
Trump's Christmas Carol
The Secret Diary of Jeremy Corbyn
#Sonnets
The Secret Diary of Boris Johnson Aged 13 ¼
The Downing Street Guide to Party Etiquette
Elon Musk (Almost) Saves The World

HONEST

The (Uncut) Memoirs of Boris Johnson

A Parody By
LUCIEN YOUNG

QUERCUS

First published in Great Britain in 2023 by

QUERCUS

Carmelite House
50 Victoria Embankment
London EC4Y 0DZ

An Hachette UK company

A CIP catalogue record for this book is available
from the British Library

HB ISBN 978 1 52943 428 6
Ebook ISBN 978 1 52943 429 3

10 9 8 7 6 5 4 3 2 1

Illustrations by Quinton Winter
Typeset by CC Book Production
Printed and bound in Great Britain by Clays Ltd, Elcograf S.p.A.

Papers used by Quercus are from well-managed forests and other responsible sources.

To my current wife, Carrie,
and however many kids I have.

PUBLISHER'S NOTE

Everything in this book is a lie. Including that.

Τὸ μὴ καλῶς λέγειν οὐ μόνον εἰς αὐτὸ τοῦτο
πλημμελές, ἀλλὰ καὶ κακόν τι ἐμποιεῖ ταῖς ψυχαῖς.

False words are not only evil in themselves,
but they infect the soul with evil.

Socrates

CONTENTS

PART ONE:

BOJO BEGINS
(1977–2007)

FOREWORD

by Nadine Dorries,
Boris's esteemed colleague and BFF

When brave, brilliant Boris asked me to provide a foreword for his memoirs, I felt honoured. Elated. #blessed. But not in the least surprised. After all, I served as his Secretary of State for Digital, Culture, Media and Sport between 2021 and 2022. Who better to sprinkle literary stardust on a major new tome? Some lefty snobs might argue that I was wholly unqualified for the role of Culture Secretary and that Boris was merely rewarding me for years of shameless toadying. That I was his gormless human shield, willing to plop down in any TV studio and defend the indefensible. But naturally, the purple-haired, septum-pierced tofu-shaggers have it all wrong. As Boris is well aware, I am a woman of taste, cultivation and elegance. I'm also tenacious, as I demonstrated by eating ostrich anus on *I'm a Celeb*.

So what can I say about the volume you hold in your hands? This is the wittiest, warmest, wisest book I have ever read (including my own *The Angels of Lovely Lane*). It combines the high drama of *Game of Thrones* with the side-splitting hilarity of a Michael McIntyre special. It's packed with Johnsonian jests and BoJo bons mots. Most importantly, it provides a corrective to the awful lies put out about him. We don't often get to hear Boris's perspective on things – the woke media (*Guardian*, BBC, *Daily Mail*) has a habit of silencing white, Old Etonian millionaires. Finally, with this book, he can defend himself against the haters.

Honest gives the reader unparalleled insight into Boris's true character (not that I needed it, being his best friend IRL). We see him during stratospheric highs and crushing lows. At times of extreme stress and overwhelming joy. As a lover, a fighter, a jester and a sage. No matter the situation, the same qualities shine through: his thoughtfulness, his integrity, his fundamental decency. These qualities go some way to explaining how one man could achieve as much as he has. Boris is too modest to say this, so allow me: he was our country's greatest post-war Prime Minister. Or pre-war. And it's not even close. He's a heroic leader. An intellectual titan. A supernova of charisma and raw sexual energy.

But as swooningly, rapturously enamoured of Boris as I am, a good friend must also be critical. BoJo isn't 100 per cent perfect. More like 99 per cent. No, 99.9. The point is, he's a man of the people, and like the people he has his flaws. He can be too generous and compassionate. Sometimes his urge to fight for

Britain is too powerful. And his blazing intellect can turn lesser mortals into gibbering wrecks. Still, these minor faults are outweighed by his accomplishments. What accomplishments, you ask? First of all: rude. Secondly, I could spend hours – days, in fact – listing the ways in which Boris has improved this country, but he asked me to keep to 600 words.

Please enjoy the following text, which I can say, without hyperbole, is more important than *On the Origin of Species*, *The Complete Works of William Shakespeare* and the Bible put together. Savour Boris's words. Treasure his ideas. And, above all, vote for him to be Prime Minister again so I can get back in the Cabinet.

The Rt. Hon. Nadine Dorries, MP for Mid Bedfordshire

Boris babes,

Hope you're happy with the above. By the way, could you call me when you get a chance? You haven't replied to my last forty-seven texts. Even though it says you've seen them. I'd hate for there to be any kind of misunderstanding between us. Anyway, hit me back.

Your biggest fan,

Nads

ADDITIONAL FOREWORD

by Jacob Rees-Mogg

Boris Johnsonus vir summo honore et ingenio est. Felix fui ad illum operari et ab eo discere. Ut notum est, homo est qui Brexit factum obtinuit et ipsum vaccinum Covidum creavit. Quisquis neget Borisem maximum ducem Britanniam semper habuisse, stultus est et delirus.

Note to Publisher: On no account should the preceding text be translated into English. If the reader is swinishly ignorant of Latin, he does not deserve my wisdom.

INTRODUCTION

What ho! 'Tis I, the blond bombshell himself, Alexander Boris de Pfeffel Johnson. You may be wondering what I've been up to since I was cruelly cast down from the heights of power. Well, I've been beavering away to make ends meet: a book deal here, an after-dinner speech there. It's hard work, mugging for a bunch of inebriated City boys in exchange for three hundred grand, but someone's got to do it. Also, I may still be MP for Uxbridge and South Ruislip – I keep meaning to check.

And yet, and yet, the Johnson heart is troubled. You see, a heap of horseshit, a gallimaufry of guff, a festering fatberg of falsehoods has been talked about my world-beating stint in Number Ten. People say I lied constantly, partied through lockdown and thoroughly demeaned the office of Prime Minister. Can you imagine?! I had hoped that these calumnies could be addressed fully in my memoirs, published by the venerable HarperCollins (£510,000 advance – ka-ching). Alas, their lawyers blanched at B-Dogg's truth bombs, and so the editorial hand came down heavily. I was dismayed to find a wealth of anecdotes expurgated, extracted and expunged.

Still, every cloud has a silver lining (just look at Covid, an excuse to throw some brilliant parties). In this case, I found myself with a whole book's worth of leftover goss. After a quick call to Quercus, *Honest: The (Uncut) Memoirs of Boris Johnson* was born. These chapters take the reader into the thatched head of the British Berlusconi, the Tory Trump, the Nero of North London, which is to say: me. They outline in bonce-combusting detail the up and downs – but mostly ups! – of my tenure in Downing Street, from Getting Brexit Done to battling the Warriors of Woke, to nearly dying because I shook too many hands. Unlike the HarperCollins book, *Honest* presents readers with the unvarnished truth (and if there's one thing I'm known for, it's telling the truth).

Yours authorially,

The Rt. Hon. A. B. D. Johnson, former PM, Hero of Ukraine, World King, four-time host of *Have I Got News for You*.

DRAMATIS PERSONAE

BORIS JOHNSON: Our hero. Luke Skywalker, John McClane and Thor all rolled into one. Would have rendered Britain a shimmering Shangri-La were it not for the civil service, Remoaners, people bent out of shape over a few parties, etc.

CARRIE JOHNSON, NÉE SYMONDS: Side chick turned main chick. A Tory media adviser who forged a series of deep friendships with middle-aged men high up in the party. Coincidentally fell in love with Boris.

DOMINIC CUMMINGS: Bald brainiac and arch-traitor. Unable to forgive Boris for his easy charm and golden locks, this dastardly Durhamite swore to destroy him.

MICHAEL GOVE: Aged schoolboy with a lightbulb for a head. Inveterate nerd, forever begging teacher to set additional homework. Repeat backstabber, like some unctuous, Scottish Brutus.

MATT HANCOCK: Grinning non-entity. Held in utter, withering contempt by Boris and everyone who has ever interacted with him. So naturally he remained in charge of Health during a once-in-a-century pandemic.

DOMINIC RAAB: Only the second most psychotic Dom in Boris's orbit. Accused by civil servants of bullying. Perhaps he Raabed them up the wrong way.

JACOB REES-MOGG: Posh sycophant. Determined to restore Britain to its Victorian heyday (sending children up chimneys). Gives his own kids bizarre names like 'Invicta' and 'Fecundus'.

NADINE DORRIES: Non-posh sycophant. Maybe a little too into Boris? Strong 'Kathy Bates in *Misery*' vibes.

JEREMY CORBYN: Bearded Communist hippie, from whose malevolent schemes (free broadband, affordable housing) Boris saves Britain.

SIR KEIR STARMER: Centrist Eeyore who gets on Boris's case about alleged parties during lockdown. His mother was a nurse and his father was a toolmaker, but he never mentions it.

DAVID CAMERON: Oleaginous PR man and establishment tool. Lit the fuse on Brexit, then sauntered away from the blast site, humming a merry tune. Eton, Oxford, Bullingdon Club – can you imagine such an upper-crust git?

THERESA MAY: Swagless Thatcher. Snatched the crown in 2016 after Boris's campaign, through no fault of his own, imploded spectacularly. Tried to restore some sanity to the Conservative party post-Brexit – big mistake!

LIZ TRUSS: Hardcore libertarian and lover of bold neckwear. Boris's immediate successor, who did him the immense favour of kamikaze-ing the UK economy and resigning within forty days. After that, no one could call him the worst Prime Minister ever.

RISHI SUNAK: Personality-free finance droid. Short-circuits whenever he meets someone whose net worth is less than seven figures. One of the horde of Judases who brought poor Boris down.

SEVERE ACUTE RESPIRATORY SYNDROME CORONAVIRUS 2 (SARS-COV-2): A plucky young illness that took the world by storm in 2020. Tried to assassinate Boris, but got roundly duffed up by his muscular white blood cells.

DONALD TRUMP: Boris if he were American and modelled himself after Gordon Gekko rather than Bertie Wooster.

JOE BIDEN: OAP (Old-Age President). Less actively deranged than Trump. Like most of his countrymen, pretends to be as Irish as the Blarney Stone. Takes a dim view of the uber-English Boris.

EMMANUEL MACRON: Wannabe Napoleon. So haughty that even the French can't stand him.

VOLODYMYR ZELENSKY: Voloddie. The Volodster. Ukrainian leader who heroically faced down Putin. Loves Boris and thinks that Boris is as brave as he is, if not braver. And he's not just saying that because he wants missiles.

THE BRITISH PUBLIC: A bunch of racist, dyspeptic lager louts who are nonetheless the salt of the earth. They loved Boris until the bitter end, and love him still, no matter what you hear from the Marxist media and woke polling firms.

TIMELINE

19 June 1964: The single most consequential date in human history, i.e. my birthday. It is not inconceivable that, in future, years will be labelled either 'BB' (Before Boris) or 'AB' (After Boris).

17 March 1988: Unbeknownst to a 23-year-old me, Carrie Symonds is born. Who would have thought those crazy kids would end up together?

24 April 1998: My first appearance on *Have I Got News for You*, in which I establish my upper-class buffoon persona. LOL, think the public, imagine this guy being in charge of anything! That would be mental!

1 May 2008: I am elected Mayor of London. Pros: plentiful opportunity for corruption, springboard to higher office. Cons: forced to interact with Cockneys.

21 February 2016: As the EU referendum kicks into gear, I am compelled to pick a side. After painstaking deliberation – over which would benefit my career most – I declare for Leave.

23 June 2016: Britain votes to exit the EU, which was definitely what I wanted to happen and not at all terrifying.

24 July 2019: Following some unpleasantness (Theresa May being Prime Minister), I enter Downing Street to whoops and hollers. The nation is united in Borismania.

12 December 2019: I secure a landslide victory at the General Election, putting me on course to rule for over a decade and fundamentally reshape British politics. In the words of Alan Cummings' character in *GoldenEye*, 'I am invincible!'

2020: Hoo boy. As I understand it, some unholy act of fornication between a bat and a pangolin results in global pestilence. Luckily, Britain has BoJo at the helm!

30 November 2021: The *Daily Mirror* reports some scurrilous nonsense about parties taking place in Downing Street during lockdown. My advisers are confident it will blow over.

7 July 2022: A billion hearts are irrevocably broken as I am forced to resign, despite my innocence on all charges. Great is the lamentation and the gnashing of teeth.

5 September 2022: My premiership draws to a close, and I leave our country in the incapable hands of Liz Truss. She proceeds to perform economic S&M with no safe word.

16 June 2023: I complete work on this, the finest, most edifying book ever written. Buy copies for all your friends! Please – I'm paying child support out the wazoo.

Projected

January 2024: Now at 0.1 per cent in the polls, the Tories tell Sunak to sling his hook and beg me to come back as Prime Minister. After careful consideration, I reluctantly agree to do so, in the national interest.

May 2024: I call a snap General Election and smash smarmy Starmer to smithereens. My unique personal connection to the voters results in 650 Conservative MPs.

2045: During my fifth consecutive term, I surpass Robert Walpole's record as the longest-serving Prime Minister. Thanks to Brexit, Britain is now a hi-tech paradise, like Wakanda but less ethnic.

2046: I step down as PM to become full-time host of *Have I Got News for You* (the BBC no longer exists, so it goes out on the Musk HoloNet). I realise that this is the job I wanted all along.

2099: I pass away at the ripe old age of 135, in the arms of my sixth wife, surrounded by several hundred children. A devastated nation pays respects by dyeing their hair blond and outlawing the use of combs. For the following year, all newborn boys are named Boris.

c. 30,000: Humanity is at war with the fearsome Vargonath. On the verge of extinction, mankind resurrects the greatest hero in Earth's history: Boris Johnson. Given a colossal robot body, Johnson annihilates the Vargonath and is proclaimed Universal Dictator. Thus begins the million-year Boris Imperium.

PRELUDE

It was early on the morning of 24 June 2016. I stood in front of a large television, surrounded by a coterie of my closest advisers. To a man (and occasional woman), we watched with bated breath. Suddenly, the following words flashed up onscreen: REFERENDUM RESULT! BRITAIN VOTES FOR BREXIT! Astonishing the whole world, the Leave campaign, of which I was the most prominent booster, had prevailed. After forty-three years, Blighty was buggering off from Brussels to face an uncertain future alone.

As the vast historical implications began to sink in, my colleagues turned to me. Boris, their eyes pleaded, grant us some words of wisdom at this seismic moment in UK politics. To which I replied: 'Oh God oh shit oh fuck. What the actual hell have we done? I didn't think for a moment that the plebs would vote for economic suicide! Those mouth-breathing pinhead twats! Oh shitty shitting shit, we haven't planned for anything! We're fucked from every conceivable position!'

Perhaps it was the lack of sleep talking. Still, to paraphrase the great Cockney thespian My Cocaine, we had only meant to blow the bloody doors off. Now the van was a smouldering wreck and flaming pieces of shrapnel were raining down and embedding in our skulls. (In this analogy, the van is Britain.) And I couldn't stop looking at that wafer-thin margin: 51.89 per cent Leave, 48.11 per cent Remain. Was there any question that my personal intervention had given Leave the edge? This meant that if the country went all *Children of Men*, the responsibility lay on my broad and manly shoulders. It's fair to say that BoJo was in a tizzy, experiencing a Brexit breakdown rather than a state of EU-phoria.

But how did I end up at this point? And where would I go from here? Don't worry, dear reader, all will be addressed. I'm just starting at a dramatic part to hook you. It's what we classicists call *in media res*.

PART ONE:

BOJO BEGINS
(1977–2007)

CHAPTER ONE

Eton My Words

In which our hero conquers an archaic and ludicrous institution, setting him up nicely for Parliament.

To paraphrase Henry Hill, the mobster protagonist of *Goodfellas*: as far back as I can remember, I always wanted to be Prime Minister. Well, originally I wanted to be 'World King', a role I invented and which has thus far proved elusive. Nonetheless, I determined at a tender age that I should be in charge. And, just as importantly, that everyone should pay me endless attention. I was to be lord of all I surveyed and cynosure of all eyes. To achieve these objectives, I would need the proper education. But which school was worthy of me? Harrow? St Paul's? Winchester? No, these were not the petri dishes in which Bacillus johnsoni would thrive. As an upper-class megalomaniac, I had only one option: Eton College.

For those of you too poor to attend (or, indeed, too female), Eton is the UK's most prestigious public school. Founded in

1440 by Henry VI, it has educated generation after generation of Britain's ruling class, instilling the virtues of snobbery and sadism. Today, some 1,300 boys board there (despite the occasional murmurs about going co-ed, the student body remains oestrogen-free). The vast majority of said children will end up in positions of power: judges, journalists, financiers. And, of course, elected officials. The roster of Old Etonians includes twenty of our fifty-seven prime ministers. These are generally the best ones, like me and Anthony Eden.

To arrive at Eton, as I did in 1977, is to commence learning a whole new language. For instance, no Etonian would call Eton 'Eton': it is simply referred to as 'School'. Boys are divvied up into Collegers and Oppidans, with the latter deriding the former for their special gowns (or 'tugs'). The masters are known as 'beaks', the matrons as 'dames'. You may have heard the term 'fagging', but don't worry: it's merely a practice wherein older boys force younger boys to act as their servants through a system of ritualised abuse.

My adjustments were social as well as linguistic. Though no slouch in the privilege department, I suddenly found myself outclassed. I was surrounded on all sides by viscounts, baronets, marquesses and foreign princes. These turbo-poshos had impressive surnames, such as Finchley-Frognal, Putterington-Dervish and Clodhopper-Pursuivant. They would regularly discuss methods for disciplining servants or which parts of

6

India their parents owned. Compared to all that, my affluent beginnings felt gritty and tough. I might as well have been wearing tracksuit bottoms and smoking a roll-up.

So as not to stand out – or, rather, to stand out on my own terms – I devised a cunning plan. I would cultivate an outrageous upper-class persona, becoming a perfect parody of my fellows. They would laugh, but in the process come to accept me. From that day forth, I tramped around the quads and playing fields, reciting half-remembered poetry in a booming tone. I stumbled and stammered my way through lessons, delighting compatriots with my irreverence. And I deliberately scruffed up my appearance, keeping my uniform askew and my hair scarecrowish. I even exchanged my name – Alexander – for a thrillingly Slavic one. Thus I effected a miraculous transformation. The caterpillar went into his chrysalis and out came the Boris butterfly.

According to psychologists, children who invent elaborate personae can become trapped in them. The defence mechanism works too well, preventing the formation of healthy adult relationships. Unable to express genuine emotion, they become hyper-ambitious and obsessed with external markers of success. Eventually, they stop discerning between fantasy and reality, between right and wrong.

Not me, though. I knew exactly what I was doing.

*

In spite of social pressures, I excelled academically. I took a particular interest in Classics, imagining myself the modern version of a Pericles or Cicero. These ancients were masters of oratory, able to whip up the rabble with their silver tongues. How I longed to do the same! I studied every rhetorical technique, from anadiplosis to zeugma. Perhaps, with enough euphemism, pleonasm and polysyndeton, I could manipulate the masses to my own ends . . .

I became immersed in Greek mythology, which appealed to some pagan part of me. Unlike that prissy do-gooder Christ, the pantheon were absolute legends. They were forever having affairs, nursing petty grievances and enacting torture on lesser beings. There was Dionysius, the life and soul of every party, and Zeus, with his pre-modern attitude to consent. I also loved the Roman god Janus, though I have no idea what I saw in this two-faced deity.

The best thing about a classical education is that hardly anyone knows Latin or Ancient Greek. You can throw out random phrases and people are guaranteed to be impressed. *Caveat emptor*! *Virgo intacta*! *Caecilius est in horto*! Admit it: you're feeling intimidated.

During my time at Eton, I made a wondrous discovery: I had been blessed with a capacious memory and a talent for improvisation. As a result, I could coast on wit and aplomb. While other,

less brainy students would prepare assiduously for each test, I could wing it and still get a high mark. In class, I would launch into a passionate disquisition on *Jude the Obscure* without reading past page five. I soon came to the conclusion that hard work was for losers. When in danger of reprimand, I would simply mug, chaff and play the clown, thereby defusing the situation.

The Masters despaired of my cavalier ways. Their reports refer to me as 'infuriatingly slapdash' and a 'dreadful little wanker'. However, I took a perverse sort of pride in being able to bluster my way through. It was all a performance: the less I knew about a subject, the more expert I sounded. Of course, I rid myself of such habits as I entered manhood. The last thing Britain needed was leaders who were ill-prepared, poorly disciplined and intellectually lazy.

On the extracurricular side, I dabbled in debate, the political society and editing the Eton *Chronicle*. My chief passion, however, was sport, that blessed simulacrum of war. I threw myself into every kind of physical activity, my hefty frame and competitive nature making short work of rivals. In addition to the usual rugby and cricket, there were such school-specific sports as Eton fives and the wall game. My favourite was Binch Prongo, a sport of incredible violence, responsible for several boy-deaths per year. Its rules are arcane and nearly impossible to describe. Essentially, players must hold a golf ball between their teeth, dislodging other players' golf balls by hitting them in the face with a brick. Meanwhile, beaks stand on the sidelines, firing harpoons at competitors. The last man standing is declared King Prong and receives medical treatment first. Binch Prongo served as a microcosm of the Eton experience: you had to win at all costs, even if it meant curb-stomping another boy, or tearing his spine out of his back.

One receives a world-class education at Eton, but more importantly, one is taught to aspire to greatness. You are never in doubt that the world is your oyster, an oyster that will most likely come with caviar and champagne. After all, you are following in the footsteps of such historic figures as Pitt the Elder, William Ewart Gladstone and George Orwell. Eton continues to pump out important men, such as yours truly, McNulty from *The Wire*, and both Spencer and Ollie from *Made in Chelsea*. Through its gates have passed world leaders, Nobel Prize recipients and Oscar winners. Which isn't to mention the famous fictional characters who went: Bertie Wooster, James Bond, Captain Hook. In my own small way, I have attempted to honour their legacies.

It is regrettable that some anarchists would like to see the place torn down. They resent Eton's central place in our national story and the dominance of Old Etonians in almost every sphere. Perhaps, they argue, there might be talented and intelligent people at other schools, people who might prove more competent at running the nation. Perhaps – so their logic goes – the levers of power should not be held exclusively by entitled men-children. This is, of course, Stalinist rubbish. It just *makes sense* for everyone important to be educated together, bonding over shared trauma and games of soggy biscuit. Floreat Etona!

If you wish to learn more about my time at Eton, I wholeheartedly recommend the excellent *Secret Diary of Boris Johnson, Aged 13¼* (also published by Quercus).

CHAPTER TWO

The First Rule of Bullingdon Club . . .

*Boris attends Oxford University, a bastion
of sober scholarship.*

The path from Eton to high political office is well-trodden and,
more often than not, runs through the University of Oxford.
Naturally, this was where I arrived to study in 1983. Well,
'study' may be stretching the truth. I was there to network,
to schmooze, to roister and carouse. I showed my face at the
occasional lecture, but the lion's share of my time was spent
on extracurricular activities. There was the Oxford Union, a
debating society in which generations of Tories have learned
to bellow, bluster and bullshit. Then, of course, there was the
Bullingdon Club.

For those not in the know, the Bullingdon is a private, all-
male 'dining club' with a membership drawn from society's
upper echelons. Less charitably, it has been described as a
bunch of posh louts who amuse themselves by tormenting the

less well-off. I appreciate that the traditions and rituals of the club may strike Joe Q. Public as outlandish. For instance, we would dress up for banquets in our uniform of bespoke navy-blue tailcoat with velvet collar, ivory silk lapel revers, brass monogrammed buttons, mustard waistcoat and sky-blue bow tie. These were expensive, but you can't put a price on style.

The feature of the club that non-members tend to fixate upon is its drunken debauchery. True, there was excessive drinking, resulting in emesis. Occasionally, strippers would be hired to entertain the braying aristocrats. And, yes, in fits of youthful exuberance, we would trash the odd pub or restaurant. At the same time, a heaping portion of rot gets talked about the Buller. Exempli gratia, the claim that members burned fifty-pound notes in front of beggars as part of an initiation ceremony. This is patently false: they were twenty-pound notes.

Anyway, it would hardly be fair to judge me for my participation. Many great men were Bullingdonians, from David Dimbleby to Cecil Rhodes. Around the time I was in the club, other members included David Cameron and George Osborne. No one would accuse them of heartless vandalism, would they?

Let me tell you about the craziest night I ever spent with the Bullingdon. It was Michaelmas term of my second year and a riotous spirit was abroad. In my rooms at Balliol, I threw on my £500 club outfit – a pretty penny in the 1980s. After an hour or so of admiring myself in the mirror, I hurried to the designated venue, a pub called The Cock and Ass. In a private function room, the usual gang had assembled: Biffy Twunkington, Xerxes Halibut, Roger Bodger-Grudgingly and others too powerful and litigious to mention. Once everyone was sitting at table, I rose to give a toast.

'Salutations, my friends. As I see it, we have two options before us. We can either spend the night discussing works of philosophy and literature. Alternatively, we can get shitfaced on Châteauneuf-du-Pape and make life hell for some povvos. Personally, I favour the latter.'

The decision was unanimous. My buddies pulled out their ceremonial crowbars and set about demolishing the place. The landlord of the Cock and Ass ran in to protest, but was quickly beaten unconscious. Yards of ale were downed and vodka enemas administered. At one point, Roger B-G leapt up on the table, yelled, 'I hate anyone who isn't a millionaire,' and promptly self-immolated. Soon after that, the night went off the rails.

Our orgy of destruction spread across Oxford. We set fire to the Bodleian Library, tarred and feathered the Vice-Chancellor, and all got Margaret Thatcher back tattoos. By 3am, we were being chased through the Botanical Gardens by some three dozen police officers. They captured us one by one, using large nets and tranquilliser darts. I awoke the next morning with a katzenjammer of Brobdingnagian proportions. Glancing around, I realised that I was not in my room at Balliol. Instead, I lay on the stone floor of a prison cell. A member of the Thames Valley Constabulary stood nearby.

'Mr A. B. D. Johnson?' he intoned. 'You've been a very naughty boy.'

A chill ran through me. There was no point denying it: my Bullingdon gear was soaked with vomit, blood and other bodily fluids. I had been caught dead to rights. I would surely be prosecuted and sent down from Oxford, killing my career before it began. Was this end of Boris Johnson?

'You and your mates did seven million pounds' worth of damage and sent dozens of people to John Radcliffe Hospital.'

I winced. What, I wondered, would be my punishment? Forty lashes? The electric chair?

'Anyway,' said the copper, 'you're free to go.'

'Pardon?' I croaked. 'What about all that stuff I did?'

The policeman shrugged.

'Normally I'd throw the book at you. But we're under strict orders not to prosecute Bullingdon lads. Can't bang up our future lords and masters, can we?'

I leapt to my feet with a 'halloo hallay'. The system worked! Within half an hour, I was back on the streets, planning our next rampage. The police were splendid about the whole thing. They even had my tailcoat cleaned.

Am I proud of what I did as a member of that time-honoured institution? No, a thousand times no. And yet I feel a deep sense of pity for the current membership, who must operate in constant fear of the iPhone lens, of having their exploits WhatsApped, TikToked and Instagrammed. In these days of the social media panopticon and woke, scolding nannyism, how are poor scions of the elite meant to get their ya-yas out? These fellows are under tremendous pressure, aware that they will inevitably occupy the heights of politics, finance, law and media. Are they not entitled to let off steam, perhaps by smashing up a fifteenth-century pub, or hurling some oik in the Cherwell?

At Eton, I had learned to slack off. At Oxford, I turned it into an art form. I was the Picasso of procrastination, the Botticelli of busking it, a half-arsed Hans Holbein. My every essay was thrown together at the last minute, often jotted while on the lavatory. In tutorials, I would vamp and extemporise to conceal a lack of reading. If I delivered my thoughts with brio, I could generally scrape through. Out came the Classics gags: 'Euripides trousers, Eumenides trousers!' 'What did Augustus say when he had a problem? Get Agrippa!' Some tutors viewed me with scorn. Others were charmed by my frantic performances. Quite right, too: I put a lot of effort into being lazy.

These experiences went on to inform my approach to government. I have never been one to sweat the small stuff. Nor

18

the medium or large stuff. Instead, I bluff and hope for the best. Whether writing an undergraduate essay, running an economy or overseeing the response to a pandemic, my motto is 'fake it till you make it'. Things will generally turn out all right. For me, if not the world.

I went to Oxford with a number of goals: getting a first, getting laid, causing more property damage than Fat Man and Little Boy combined. Most importantly, I wanted to be President of the Oxford Union. This position has proved a springboard to many a storied political career. I was determined to climb the greasy pole in record time, so I threw my hat in the ring. On the first attempt, I ran as a standard-issue Old Etonian Tory. To my bewilderment, this turned out to have limited appeal: I was soundly defeated. For the next attempt, I recruited a small army of stooges to aid in my campaign. This included Frank Luntz, a Yankee dweeb who went on to be a pollster, and Michael Gove, some chap from Aberdeen who never amounted to anything. I won their support by making wild promises I had no intention of keeping, a technique I would return to in later life. I was duly elected, having abandoned my political convictions and run as a middle-of-the-road liberal. Which is also how I became the Mayor of London.

In May of my fourth year, with finals fast approaching, I decided to get serious about my studies. I burned the midnight oil and put in literally hours of work. I sat my exams, filling the paper with amusing digressions and clever puns about Thucydides. Despite this, I was awarded a 2:1 rather than my expected first. I was anguished, affronted, utterly apoplectic. Why would they give a second-class degree to an obviously first-class boy? I collared the Master of Balliol and demanded to know the meaning of this insult. He suggested I should have applied myself earlier. What did he expect me to do? Revise, like some girly swot? No, the quality of my work was not at issue. I was an early victim of cancellation by woke dons.

CHAPTER THREE

EC Does It

In which Boris makes a name for himself on the continent.

Picture me now at twenty-four, striding through the streets of Brussels, a Belgian waffle in one hand and a tankard of witbier in the other. The year was 1989 and I was in the prime of my life. I was bursting with vim, vigour, piss and vinegar. And, above all, spunk. *The Daily Telegraph* had hired me to cover the European Commission, despite my lack of journalistic experience. As a nascent member of the Fourth Estate, I was eager to make my mark on the world. Not through piercing reportage, but rather by generating as much noise and stink as possible. To that end, I would wear loud Bermuda shorts and zip around the city in a bright red Alfa Romeo, causing consternation among the stuffy Eurocrats.

I loved living à Bruxelles. This may surprise liberals who view me as a xenophobe, but it's true. I spent part of my boyhood in nearby Uccle, so I was proficient in French, allowing me to enjoy the city to the fullest. I would go for long walks in the Parc du Cinquantenaire, shop in Les Galeries Royales Saint-Hubert and take the occasional day trip to Bruges. To freely live and work in a European city is a beautiful thing: I believe every young person should have the opportunity.

For some, the role of a journalist is to report the truth without fear or favour, thereby comforting the afflicted and afflicting the comfortable. I saw things rather differently. In my view, the role of a journalist was to print as much codswallop as the public would swallow. Young Boris wasn't about to take a course on journalistic ethics, or spend his every waking hour establishing facts. Facts are the preserve of the unimaginative.

I knew the *Telegraph* readership – average age 103 – despised Eurocrats as much as they loved having second homes in Provence. To win the old coots over, I would need to spin yarns of Brussels-based perfidy and incompetence. So I set about excoriating the EC and its villainous president, Jacques Delors. In my telling, Europe was an aspiring super-state, determined to stomp on British sovereignty and ban Beef Wellington. Here are some of my headlines from the time:

EC STIFFENS RULES ON VIAGRA

METHANE TAX FOR WIND-BREAKING BRITS

BRUSSELS BUST-UP: BOOBS TOO BIG,
SAYS COMMISSION

Were any of these stories true? Not, perhaps, in the sense of being accurate. The more important truth is that they garnered attention. I was tossing bombs and putting a cat among the pigeons. Or, to combine metaphors, putting a cat strapped with Semtex among the pigeons, then squeezing a remote detonator.

There are those who argue that my stories popularised anti-EC sentiment. That I was patient zero for Euroscepticism, sowing the seeds of UKIP and Farage. I really couldn't say. What I do know is that my columns wowed Conservatives back home. If you deplored Delors, I was your favourite hack. I even won famous admirers. One day I received a phone call and was thrilled to recognise the voice on the other end. It was husky, forceful and very, very sexy.

'Hello Boris, this is Margaret Thatcher.'

'Madam Prime Minister. To what do I owe this honour?'

'I just wanted to say how much I enjoy your dispatches. They have inspired me to take a harder line against Delors. Ghastly little frog . . . '

'I'm glad to count you as a reader,' I stammered. 'Thanks for taking the time to call.'

'Not at all,' replied Mrs T. 'By the way, Boris, have you ever thought of going into politics?'

Once or twice, I admitted.

'Oh, but you must! I can tell from your writing that you would make a wonderful Prime Minister – much better than me. Also, you sound really fit. What are you wearing right now?'

I am a gentleman, so I will draw a veil over the rest.

By 1994, I had hit a wall. I was running out of fabrications, having accused Eurocrats of wanting to standardise condom sizes, regulate the curve of bananas and force women to return their old sex toys. The Commission hires teams of sniffers to analyse manure? I already used that one. Euro notes make you impotent? Ditto. So I decided it was time to return to my beloved Blighty. The Brussels gig had been fun, but I was ready for new challenges. No longer would I lie about Europe to advance my career.

CHAPTER FOUR

Johnson on Display

Fame beckons Boris.

Consider, if you will, the columnist. Britain is blessed with more columnists per capita than any other country. From Giles Coren to Julie Burchill to Richard Littlejohn, this land bristles with opinion-mongers. They are world-renowned for their sensitivity, intellectual depth and commitment to excellence. They are rigorous in their truth-telling and would never pull stuff out of their arse to meet a deadline. Also, if you want ten million articles attacking trans people, the British columnist has you covered.

Upon returning to London, I had the honour to join this lofty caste. Max Hastings, the editor of the *Telegraph*, promoted me to Assistant Editor and Chief Political Columnist. As a columnist, I had one tremendous advantage: I didn't really believe in anything. Other political writers would waste precious time figuring out where they stood on the issues. I dispensed with such footling. You name the position and I would argue it to the hilt. One week I would plead for the conservation of the noble badger, the next I would call for a nationwide cull. Unencumbered by principles, I could focus on my true passion: showing off my vocabulary and making hilarious jokes. It is true that, from time to time, my language became somewhat piquant. The PC brigade object to my use of phrases like 'tank-topped bumboys' and 'piccaninnies with watermelon smiles'. However, these are taken out of context. Don't bother checking the context: I promise it's fine.

My star was in the ascendent, but it only went supernova when I was asked to appear on humorous BBC panel show *Have I Got News for You*. I immediately recognised the opportunity. HIGNFY was a big deal: it would let me reach beyond the moustachioed colonels who read the *Telegraph*. By putting in an amusing performance, I could achieve a measure of celebrity, boosting my journalistic career and setting myself up for Parliament. With this in mind, it was a fired-up Boris that arrived at the London Studios. Makeup girls dabbed at me with brushes and the hair department did their utmost. Assuming my seat onstage, I restored my hair to its previous dishevelment. I was on Paul Merton's team, facing off against Ian Hislop and Janet Street-Porter (yet another columnist). Presiding over festivities was the show's suave host, Angus Deayton.

I experienced a twinge of stage fright as the studio lights

came up. However, my nerves dissipated when I received my first proper laugh. I soon realised that clowning around in front of cameras was well within my repertoire. Like Liam Neeson in *Taken*, I had a very particular set of skills – here was the perfect context in which to deploy them. I gurned, stammered and acted befuddled, peppering my speech with Wodehousian phraseology. The studio audience ate it up. Who was this plummy anachronism? And why was he so endearing? Imagine if the tousle-headed toff was in charge of things! Wouldn't that be hilarious?

Returning to the green room, I was set upon by eager producers. They gushed over my barnstorming performance and pleaded with me to come back soon. I feigned reticence, but the limelight was impossible to resist. I would appear on the programme twice more as a contestant and four times as guest host.* Each time I did, it was ratings dynamite. Like a televisual King Midas, everything I touched turned to gold. I crushed again and again, eliciting raucous laughter with my upper-class-twit persona. Soon I was being offered spots on other shows: *Top Gear*, *Parkinson*, *Breakfast with Frost*. BoJo had hit the big time.

I truly believe my political career would not have flourished

---

* Angus Deayton would be dismissed after the *News of the World* reported that he had taken cocaine and had sex with prostitutes. Imagine being brought down by such a meagre scandal! It seems that panel show hosts are held to a higher standard than mayors or prime ministers.

without HIGNFY. The show gave me a direct line to the viewing public, allowing me to charm and disarm them. The more Messrs Merton, Hislop and Deayton derided me, the more beloved I became. While other politicians would recoil from their jests and japes, I received them on the chin. I was good old Boris, who didn't take himself too seriously. I wonder if the satirists behind the scenes feel conflicted. Rather than spoofing me to oblivion, they enabled my ascent. Then again, perhaps 'Prime Minister Boris' is the ultimate spoof.

With the increase in my public profile came a sea change in my day-to-day life. All of a sudden, I was recognised wherever I went. Buxom beauties bounded up to me and said they admired my column. I had a stock response, but it would be too vulgar to print. My fanbase was broader than one might expect for a paid-up Tory toff. There were BoJo stans of all colours, creeds and class backgrounds. I would be clapped on the shoulder by a Bangladeshi shopkeeper, then embraced by a Nigerian cleaning lady. I would pass a building site and hear cries of 'LOL, Boris, legend!' They had all seen me on their TV screens and decided I wasn't as bad as the rest of my ilk.

Yes, I was beloved across the political spectrum, something I knew would never change.

CHAPTER FIVE

A Cock and Bull Tory

Our hero slouches into Parliament as a part-time MP.

Around the turn of the millennium, I sensed that destiny was upon me. It was time to transcend the commentariat and start my career as a Member of Parliament. But to enter the Commons, I needed a seat, ideally a safe Conservative one. Which constituency would boast Boris as its representative? Chaffinch? Blumpton South? Little Frothingham-on-the-Wold?

Eventually I settled upon Henley, an affluent slice of Oxfordshire that is as Tory as can be. Beyond it hosting a regatta, I didn't know the first thing about the place, nor had I any intention of learning. What were they going to do, not make me MP? I was the guy from *Have I Got News for You*! Lo and behold, the selection committee succumbed to my charms and I was on my way.

Along came the 2001 general election. As you no doubt recall, the shiny-pated Yorkshireman William Hague was routed by

Tony Blair, who hadn't yet gone full supervillain. It was a catastrophic night for the Conservatives, but I couldn't have cared less: I was elected with a proudly tumescent majority of 8,500. Take a bow, Boris Johnson MP.

Soon I found myself amid the Gothic grandeur of the Palace of Westminster. I was one of just twenty-six new Tory MPs. This suited me fine, as it meant less competition. Other members of the 2001 intake included my Eton-and-Oxford rival David Cameron and a smirky lordling called George Osborne. I treated them with equanimity, confident that both would fall by the wayside.

So there I was in the mother of parliaments, legislating on matters that affected sixty million people. Was I happy? Was I hell. You see, I faced an unavoidable fact: being an MP is boring. It entails early mornings, hours of drudgery and an avalanche of mind-numbing policy papers. One may be placed on a standing committee, forced to go through neverending bills, like some legislative Sisyphus. Worst of all is constituency work. MPs are meant to hold 'surgeries', in which the yokels that elected them can come and have a chat. I would rather undergo actual surgery, without anaesthetic, on my genitals.

I comforted myself with the prospect of advancement. Surely I would receive a ministerial role in which to showcase my considerable talents? I was informed that new MPs were expected to get their heads down and put in the time. Sod that, I thought. I wasn't some Shropshire bumpkin who worked his way up from councillor – I was Boris Johnson, for goodness' sake! I should have been offered a Cabinet position on my first day. And not one of the piddly-widdly ones, like Northern Ireland or Environment.

I'm afraid there's no sugarcoating it: serving the people was an almighty drag. I fell into a torpid stupor (or, indeed, a stupid torpor), with concomitant physiological effects. My once lithe anatomy grew flabby and stout. For this reason, I took up jogging, squeezing in sweaty half-hours wherever I could. I soon felt the cardiovascular benefits, as my body tautened to its present muscularity. Perhaps you've seen footage of me barrelling along like Pheidippides, wearing some jaw-droppingly odd ensemble. In lieu of running gear, I don whatever items come to hand, e.g. dress shoes, a formal shirt and a skull-and-crossbones bandana. Not that I'm trying to draw attention to myself.

I also began cycling, a pastime for which I am rightly famed. It brought me great joy to whizz around Westminster, imagining myself as various historical figures: Genghis Khan, Napoleon, Dracula. I would careen through crowds of hapless pedestrians, exclaiming 'Watch out! World King coming through!' I have never been someone who feels unduly hindered by traffic laws. Or any laws, come to think of it.

*

I soon tired of my parliamentary responsibilities and rarely turned up to vote. If I wasn't doing the job of MP, how did I spend my time? Well, I was busy with my second job. And my third job. And my fourth. The basic MP's salary in 2001 was a paltry £51,822, so I had little choice but to pursue alternative income streams. Chief among these was my role as editor of *The Spectator* magazine. This was jolly good fun, allowing me to commission pieces from interesting chaps like Taki, who held forth on 'black hoodlums' and 'bongo-bongo land'. On top of that were my *Telegraph* pieces, various television appearances and a motoring column for *GQ*. Poop poop!

Then there were my literary endeavours. Like Disraeli before me, I decided to be both a top-flight politician and a serious novelist. The result was *Seventy-Two Virgins*, a satirical tale of dastardly Arab terrorists trying to blow up the Palace of Westminster. This was reviewed as an 'effortlessly brilliant page-turner' by the *Telegraph* (coincidentally my employer). They were certainly right about it being effortless: I must have knocked the thing out in a few days. Not that one could tell, given the book's exquisite prose, sociopolitical insight and richly drawn characters. How many authors would describe a woman as a 'mega-titted six-footer', or Arabs as having 'hook noses and hairy black eyebrows that [join] in the middle'?

The best thing about doing an absurd number of jobs is that

one can always justify screwing up. Column filed late? I was busy in Parliament. Missed a vote? I was filing my column. Also, I had a surfeit of alibis when the wife asked where I was last night.

CHAPTER SIX

Political Erectness Gone Mad

BoJo's mojo gets ladies a-go-go.

It behoves me at this point to address, shall we say, the elephant in the room. A great deal has been written over the years about my somewhat baroque love life. The papers love to chronicle each and every one of my supposed affairs. They spill as much ink as I do seed. Allegedly. So let's discuss Bonking Boris, the Commons Casanova.

It is true that I am a man of powerful urges. BJ is remorselessly red-blooded, with an eye (and other parts) for the ladies. This priapic predisposition has got me in trouble many a time. Most notably, I was sacked by then-Conservative leader Michael Howard for lying about an affair with my *Spectator* colleague Petronella Wyatt. Unkind souls have suggested that I am a love rat. That all I care about is pleasing my Right Honourable member. That I would betray any trust and risk any relationship for the sake of a momentary buzz. Which is, needless to say, twaddle, bosh and stultiloquence in excelsis.

The fact is, the fair sex has always been drawn to my unique physique and turbocharged pheromones. They become crazed with lust, a danger to themselves and others. As much as I respect the institution of marriage, it would be selfish – cruel, even – to deny them.

So yes, I may, very occasionally, have strayed beyond the bounds of matrimony. These were moments of madness (which sometimes went on for several years). But it was good, healthy fun, and no one got hurt. Except my wife at the time. And quite a few of the women.

Anyway, such are the follies of youth. And middle age. I am now older, wiser and very happily married. As I often assure Carrie, I would never cheat on her. That said, I was cheating when we got together, so she should probably watch her back.

I know what you're thinking: Boris, how do you do it? How do you bed these ravishing mega-babes? Sure, you're a handsome guy, with your resplendent mane and manly jowls. In fact, you're a dishevelled adonis. But what accounts for your astronomical hit-rate? Well, part of it is luck: I am simply adept in matters rumpoid and pumpoid. Nonetheless, there are certain techniques, certain clever tricks, that I have found useful. As a favour to less naturally gifted males, here are Boris Johnson's Patented Seduction Tips.

1. Grooming: avoid at all costs. What women want is a man who looks like he sleeps in his car.
2. Confidence is sexy. It therefore follows that the more confident you are, the sexier. Approach one's target crumpet and announce, 'I am your god! Kneel before me!'
3. LLL: Ladies Love Latin. Hit her with *amo, amas, amat* and you'll be conjugating in no time. If you know your declensions, she won't decline coitus.
4. Always mix business with pleasure. Is the object of your desire a subordinate? Suggest that you could help with her career, were it not for this tightness in your trousers . . .
5. If at first you don't succeed, lie, lie again. Lying is as essential to seduction as it is to gaining political office, so let rip with the porkies. Why not tell her that you're an astronaut spy, or that you won the Nobel Prize for cunnilingus?

Of course, one could follow the above rules to the letter and still strike out. What really helps is being important. Chicks will flock to a mayor, say, or a head of government. Power is the ultimate aphrodisiac. It even works on me: sometimes I get aroused when glimpsing myself in the mirror. Actually, I might have to take a five-minute break from writing . . .

Believe me, I could fill a third volume of memoirs with my various dalliances and assignations. It would probably sell double the copies this book does, titillating readers and forcing them to take frequent wank-breaks. It could be called *Fifty Shades of Blond*. Alas, my honour forbids me. A gentleman doesn't kiss and tell, or indeed lay pipe and tell. On the other hand, this chapter is running short, so forget all that. Perhaps I can get away with it if I keep the women anonymous . . .

One particularly erotic episode saw me backstage at the O2 Arena. A certain platinum-selling American singer was performing there, and I had been told she was eager to meet. Brushing past a phalanx of bodyguards, I entered her dressing room. There she sat, naked save for a carefully positioned guitar. Though she was almost half my age, our chemistry was immediate and overwhelming.

'Boris,' she said, 'thanks for coming.'

'I haven't. At least not yet.'

She smiled, impressed by my suave repartee.

'You know, I've been with British guys before: Tom Hiddleston, Harry Styles. But never one as macho as you.'

It was clear this sultry siren had BoJo fever. Fortunately, I was able to provide the cure. I won't divulge the young songstress's name. Suffice it to say we were tailor-made for each other and she was swift to take me to bed.

Another time, I was in Milan for an economic summit, which

40

happened to coincide with that city's famed Fashion Week. Who should I run into at the hotel bar but a certain US model with a confoundingly Polish surname?

'Oh em gee!' she cried. 'Boris Johnson! You're the hottest world leader – way hotter than that limp dick Justin Trudeau.'

'Anonymous,' I replied. 'What a pleasure to finally meet. I've admired you since the "Blurred Lines" music video.'

She grinned, sex-wantingly.

'So you're familiar with my body . . . of work?'

'Indeed. I enjoyed your performance in 2014's *Gone Girl*, and I respect your brand of pop feminism.'

'Thank you, Prime Minister. Would you like to come up to my room for . . . coffee?'

'I'd rather have sexual intercourse.'

'Even better.'

Again, I will protect the identity of my inamorata. Though 'inamorata' sounds a lot like her nickname.

Perhaps my steamiest encounter was with a certain A-list movie star. We met at a glitzy event and her horniness was palpable. Seriously, I was able to palp it. We went straight to Heathrow, jumped aboard a private jet and flew to the Bahamas for a solid week of salami-hiding. We feasted on one another from dawn till dusk, taking hanky-panky to new heights. Were there a venereal version of the *Guinness Book of World Records*, we would feature heavily. I had more carnal knowledge than a Professor of Sex at Fuckingham University.

Once seven days had elapsed, I was ready to return to London.

'Have a nice life,' I told the actress, shaking her warmly by the hand. But there was a sting in the tale. My bedmate had, as the young people say, caught feelings. As I attempted to leave, she fell to her knees and begged, 'Marry me, Boris, please! Without you by my side, I can't go on starring in films like *Wolf of Wall Street* and *Suicide Squad*!'

To which I replied, 'I'm sorry, Margot Robbie,* we're through.'

She was far from the only celeb who wanted to put a ring on it. But I was a rolling stone and had to keep on moving. Also, I was already married.

---

* Blast, I meant to keep her anonymous. Ah well, I can go back and edit later.

PART TWO:

THE INEVITABLE ASCENT
(2007–2019)

CHAPTER SEVEN

Capital Offences

In which our hero becomes King of the Cockneys.

The year was 2007. It was a wild time. Rihanna and Jay-Z rode high in the charts with 'Umbrella'. A subprime mortgage crisis was about to wreak havoc on global finances. Most significantly, a certain MP for Henley was gearing up for his next great adventure. Having long since tired of being a small fish in the Commons, I set my eye on the snugger pond of City Hall. Boris Johnson, Mayor of London: that had a ring to it. I could fill my days with ribbon-cuttings and self-aggrandising speeches, becoming MC for the greatest city on Earth. Also, I suspected I might get to wear a chain, or a sash with 'MR MAYOR' written on it.

The figure standing in my way was Ken Livingstone, the sitting Labour mayor (hang on, was he standing or sitting?). A canny operator and ardent Trotskyist, Livingstone could not have been more different from me. And I don't just mean his comprehensive education and council house accent. He was a creature steeped in municipal politics, while my interest in London was limited to Westminster, Kensington and Chelsea and – at a stretch – Islington. He had improved the transport system, secured the 2012 Olympics and dealt with terrorist attacks, while I was primarily known for panel show buffoonery and extramarital affairs. After eight years, though, Londoners were tired of their hammer-and-sickle-wielding overlord. They needed someone who could cheer them up, who would go about with flies undone and get stuck on zip lines. I was their man!

The mayoral campaign was hard fought. I largely eschewed policies, focusing instead on good vibes. My message was simple: 'Boris as mayor? Wouldn't that be a laugh!' Livingstone's team pulled a series of dirty tricks, by which I mean accurately reporting things I had said and done. Their goal was to portray me – me! – as some kind of amoral, philandering bigot. However, these below-the-belt antics were all in vain. Come election day – 1 May 2008 – the 'LOL, Boris' tendency won out. I was now charged with the wellbeing of eight million citizens, mostly because voters thought it would be funny. Democracy is indeed a strange and wonderful thing.

What would be my focus as mayor? Getting house prices under control? Improving living standards for the average Londoner? Making the Thames less brown? No, no and no. Instead, my overriding passion was to build colossal eyesores using the public purse. For example, the ArcelorMittal Orbit, a tangle of red steel around a viewing platform, or the Emirates Air Line, the world's most expensive cable car. It felt majestic to conjure structures with a wave of my hand (and the help of corporate sponsors). My name was Bozymandias, mayor of mayors: look on my works, ye mighty, and despair!

As well as these stellar contributions to urban life, there were many projects that never materialised. There was a pedestrian 'Garden Bridge' over the Thames, which cost the taxpayer £43 million before being scrapped. There was Boris Island, a proposed airport in the Thames estuary that would have cost £47.3 billion. Then there were the wheezes I kept secret. Private submarines to ferry VIPs down the river. A giant seesaw balanced on the Gherkin. The Johnson ziggurat, on top of which would be a shrine to the World King. Moaning Minnies will say that I turned the capital into a white elephant graveyard, littering the landscape with vanity projects and grotesque follies. Furthermore, that I wrecked the London skyline by letting rapacious developers put up a series of high-rises. But what's the point of being mayor if you can't have fun?

Eccentric landmarks weren't the only thing on which I splashed the cash: I also spent £320,000 on water cannons. Gallingly, Home Secretary Theresa May then banned their use for crowd-control. My successor as mayor, Sadiq Khan,

47

complained about being saddled with them. This demonstrates his lack of imagination. Had he built the Garden Bridge, perhaps the cannons could have been used to water it. Who knows? And who cares? It wasn't my money being spent.

In 2010, the long reign of New Labour drew to a close. As a true-blue Tory, I should have been overjoyed. Alas, the Conservatives were led at the time by one David Cameron. Cameron was an apple-cheeked aristocrat born with a platinum spoon in his mouth, and he and I had been rivals since our days at Eton. We both arrived in Parliament as part of the small 2001 intake, but I languished while he climbed the ranks. Most importantly, he got a first at Oxford, while I was slapped with a 2:1. I am convinced that this was the result of cheating or some conspiracy.

Now the guy was going to be Prime Minister. I consoled myself with the knowledge that D-Cam could only form a government thanks to the wet blanket brigade, i.e. the Lib Dems. He was a toothless Dracula, with Nick Clegg as his Renfield. Still, young Davy had leapfrogged me, and it stung. I privately swore to bring the ham-faced tosser down. Maybe through – I don't know – a referendum of some kind.

CHAPTER EIGHT

Arcuri-ous

*Boris serves a second term as mayor, has an entirely
innocent relationship with an American businesswoman,
then bails in the hope of becoming PM.*

There is an odious accusation made against mayors, namely that holders of the office are uniquely susceptible to corruption. I can honestly say that I was a model of propriety throughout my tenure. I crossed every 't' and dotted every 'i', especially when I was writing 'tits'. Despite this, the media kept on concocting scandals. Most fanciful was the notion that I conducted an affair with American tech entrepreneur, former DJ and model Jennifer Arcuri. Of course this is absurd. I had already been embroiled in several sex scandals by that point, which had severely hindered my career. What kind of dick-brained lunatic would carry on again as Mayor of London?

No, my relationship with Jennifer was as platonic as the Allegory of the Cave. She was a blonde bombshell, doe-eyed and buxom. I was a five-star stud with testosterone coming out of my ears. But never once did we succumb to temptation. Instead, we enjoyed a connection based on intellectual curiosity. It was a very normal friendship, the kind that blossoms between a middle-aged father-of-several and a woman twenty-one years his junior. We would spend long, pleasurable nights at her flat, discussing Plutarch, Flaubert and Dostoyevsky, pants firmly on. It was pure coincidence that I neglected to mention our friend-ship to my then-wife Marina.

Certain muck-rakers have raised their eyebrows at the fact that Jennifer was awarded £126,000 of public funds during this time. Or that she accompanied me on overseas trade missions. Nothing to see there, I'm afraid. I was simply motivated by a profound interest in her company, Innotech. I have no idea what the company actually did, but just listen to that name. Innovation *and* technology! Clearly they were up to something impressive. Do these journalists object to the innovating of technologies? If so, they should cast their smartphones and laptops into the sea and live as mud-caked Luddites.

It is a shame, admittedly, that Ms Arcuri has given a number of interviews describing our non-existent affair in detail. I assure you, dear reader, nothing untoward happened. But if it did, it would have been the most orgasmic experience of her, or any woman's, life.

*

The crowning achievement of my mayoralty was, without a doubt, the 2012 Olympics. This event may have been secured by my predecessor, but like his bicycle hire scheme, I was determined to put my name on it. As a classicist, it thrilled me that the Games originated in my beloved Ancient Greece. And the attention . . . Oh, the attention! The eyes of the world – which is roughly 16 billion eyes – would be on London, and I would be in the front row, waving a Union Jack and gurning to camera. Forget Mo Farah, Andy Murray and Rebecca Adlington: the star of the London Olympics would be Boris Johnson.

This was never reported in the press, but I made vigorous efforts to join Team GB. I have always been a fine athlete, from decimating opponents in the Eton wall game, to that time I rugby-tackled a Japanese child. When you combine that with my renowned cycling ability, it only seemed fair they should find a slot for me. I called up Sebastian Coe to give him the good news:

'Sebster old chum, I'm in. Boris wants to take home gold. Put me on the team.'

For some reason, Lord Coe seemed nonplussed. People I speak to are often nonplussed when they should be plussed.

'Boris,' he said, 'this is rather a surprise. In what event would you be competing?'

'Oh, that doesn't matter. I don't need a glamorous one. I'm fine with javelin, canoeing, volleyball. Hell, I'd even take shot-put.'

There was a pause, then Seb spoke again.

'I'm afraid it's a no. Firstly, you would be guaranteed to embarrass yourself and the country. Secondly, it would be unfair to the athletes who have worked all their lives to get to this point.'

'Pole vault? Come on, you can definitely give me pole vault . . . '

'Boris, you're not up to the job.'

To which I shot back, brilliantly: 'I've been a journalist, a novelist, an MP and a mayor without ever being up to it. Why should this be any different?'

Despite the rhetorical checkmate, my request was denied.

A great preoccupation of mine was the Games' opening ceremony. The Chinese had thrown down the gauntlet in 2008, with the astonishing display of synchronised drumming that opened the Beijing Olympics. We Brits would have to pull something even more impressive from our bowler hat. The role of artistic director of the opening ceremony was given to one Danny Boyle. As you may recall, Boyle is responsible for *Trainspotting*, a film about young Caledonians indulging in their national pastime of heroin. Upon his appointment, I called him into my office at City Hall.

'Listen, Boyle,' I intoned, 'I have nothing but respect for your oeuvre – *Shallow Hal*, *Scumbag Millionaire*, both tremendous. That said, I feel this project could benefit from collaboration . . .'

I proceeded to outline my concepts for an audiovisual extravaganza. How about a state-of-the-art fireworks display spelling out the mayor's name? Or an all-female chorus line, each equipped with a Boris face mask? Imagine: a thousand sexy Borises performing high kicks. There were plans for a sketch featuring James Bond and the Queen. I approved of this, but did Bond have to be played by Daniel Craig? They had already taken the step of casting a blond 007: why not go blonder?

In the end, Boyle junked all of my world-beating ideas, opting for some lefty piffle about the benefits of multiculturalism and the foundation of the NHS. Despite this, the Games were a resounding success. Team GB did the nation proud, winning a trove of gold medals (though not as many as they would have, had I been allowed to compete). People often cite that opening ceremony as the last time they felt proud to be British. They must be forgetting Brexit and my landslide election.

Following the Olympics, I entered something of a malaise. As mayor, I had solved all of London's problems. The capital was now a wonderful place for everyone. The streets were sparkling clean, the air fresh and pine-scented, the populace unfailingly polite. What lofty heights were left for Boris to scale? Like Sherlock Holmes, my mind rebelled at stagnation.

Flash forward to 2014. I was cycling down the Old Kent Road, whizzing about like a non-steroidal Lance Armstrong.

As I tarried at a red light, I became cognisant of a figure to my left. It was a tiny, wizened old man, visibly Cockney, eyes bright with the rough-hewn wisdom of the working class. Clearly he had recognised me, despite the cycle helmet obscuring my trademark profusion of blond.

''Ere, Mistah Johnson,' said this Man on the Street. 'Do us a fave-ah. Return to the 'Ouse of Commons so you can be PM. We need a leadah 'oo cares, not some posh twat like Cameron.'

'My good man,' I replied, 'I wish I could help. But to become Prime Minister, one must be a sitting MP. I'm merely a humble mayor.'

'Might I take the liber'ee of makin' a suggestion, guv'nor?'

'By all means.'

'You could always rahn in the safe Conservative seat of Uxbridge and South Ruislip. We know there'll be an election next year, fanks to the Fixed-term Parliaments Act 2011.'

I chuckled appreciatively.

'My dear, simple Cockney friend, would that it were so easy. The fact is, I've promised to see out my term, which ends in 2016. As a man of my word, I couldn't possibly stand.'

The pensioner became grave, looking like some tribune of the people.

'I 'ave one question: does your word outweigh the 'opes and dreams of every man, woman and child in this country? Because 65 million people out there need Boris Johnson to be

PM. To grant 'em a brighter future and make 'em proud once more to be Bri'ish. Compared to that, 'oo gives an 'oot about some bleedin' promise?'

'My God, you're right. But won't people think me a cynical careerist?'

My Cockney interlocutor shook his head, voice trembling with emotion.

'No sane person could think that, Mr Mayor. Or dare I say . . . Prime Minister?'

I cycled off, his glottally-stopped words ringing in my ears. I was astounded to have chanced upon someone so wise, so earthy, so totally non-fictional. Someone who argued for all the things I wanted to do already. By the time I got home and hung up my helmet, my mind was made up. I would re-enter Parliament and seize my rightful place as First Lord of the Treasury. And if that involved screwing over David Cameron, then so be it. As Dr Johnson nearly remarked: when a man is tired of being Mayor of London, he should run for PM.

CHAPTER NINE

Brexistential Crisis

Wherein a momentous choice is made.

And so we come to the part you've all been waiting for. To paraphrase Salt-N-Pepa, let's talk about Brex, baby! Some commentators believe that I will be remembered primarily for my role in Brexit. I prefer to think it will be for my panel show appearances and Steve McQueen levels of cool. But the EU referendum of 2016 is a key component of the BoJo saga. How did the UK arrive at this ruction? Read on, dear seeker of knowledge, and all shall be made clear.

For years, the Conservatives had been deeply divided on Britain's membership of the European Union, with the party's Eurosceptic wing becoming ever more boisterous. Meanwhile, we were being harried on our right flank by the insurgent UKIP, led by scotch-egg-burp-in-human-form Nigel Farage. Spooked, Cameron responded by promising a vote on EU membership if the Tories won the next election. May 2015 duly came and

Labour was sunk by Ed Miliband's weird sandwich-eating technique. The Conservatives achieved a majority and would no longer be held back by mopey Nick Clegg and his yellow wets. The referendum was on like Donkey Kong.

At the time, conventional wisdom held that the country would vote to Remain. Why risk years of turmoil for the nebulous benefits of going it alone? What happened next would split the nation in two and divide the population between quinoa-chomping Remainiacs and gammon-headed Brexiteers. It would pit parents against children, husbands against wives, friends against friends. It would also set off a chain of events that landed me in Downing Street, so was clearly worth it.

As the UK's most popular, charismatic and widely fancied politician, I was naturally courted by both Leave and Remain. In a tight contest, each side knew the BoJo bump could make all the difference. Particularly conscious of this was David Cameron. Allow me to present, verbatim, a phone call I received from the Prime Minister in January 2016.

DC: Hullo Boris. Thanks for taking the time. I know you're terribly busy.

BJ: Well well well, if it isn't Cameron Minor. How you doing, young fellow-me-lad?

DC: Not too well, I'm afraid. That's why I'm calling. You see, this referendum has me rather worried. If Leave prevails, it will mean the end of my premiership.

BJ: Mm, yes, that would be tragic . . .

DC: So I was wondering whether you could help me out. As fellow OEs, brothers of the Bullingdon and, dare I say, friends?

BJ: [Non-committal noise]

DC: I want you to declare your support for Remain. That would be just the fillip we need.

BJ: Sorry, Prime Minister, but no can do. I'm still wrestling with the myriad implications, weighing economic concerns against issues of sovereignty, et cetera.

DC: Are you bollocks! You're just working out what's best for Boris!

BJ: David, are you impugning my honour?

[Pause]

DC: No. No, of course not. Look, I shouldn't have said that. I'm under a lot of pressure right now. Between the referendum and this nonsense about me at the Piers Gaveston . . .

BJ: Ah yes. Pig's Head Revisited. The porking PM. David Ham-eron and his porcine paramour.

DC: Well, quite. So will you back Remain?

BJ: And save your bacon? I can't make any promises.

DC: Please, Boris, everybody loves you! They won't listen to me – I'm just a shiny-faced mediocrity!

BJ: Dave . . .

DC: What can I give you? A peerage? The Foreign Office? You name the price.

BJ: This isn't about ambition.

DC: Fine, I admit you're smarter than me! Always have been. The only reason I did better than you at Oxford is I cheated!

BJ: Prime Minister—

DC: You're hotter, too. My wife fancies the pants off you. In fact, Sam only has sex with me if I put on a blond wig and do an impression.

BJ: David, I have too much respect for your office to allow this to continue. Goodbye.

DC: I'll let you kick me in the arse. As many times as you want. It can be in public. I—

End of call.

Again, this is all verbatim. But Cameron was wasting his breath: for me, the choice between Leave and Remain was a profound moral judgement. I could not be swayed by threats or promises. Especially from a man who allegedly stuck his penis in a decapitated swine.

In February 2016, I announced my support for the Leave campaign via a column in the *Daily Telegraph*. As is widely known, I also wrote a second column, one that argued Britain should Remain. A cynic might suggest I was making personal calculations. This could not be further from the truth. Allow me to explain, with perfect candour, how I came to my historic decision.

It was late one evening and my *Telegraph* column was overdue. The editor had been on the phone, howling at me, demanding copy on his desk. Yet I was frozen. Paralysed. Caught, like Buridan's ass, between two choices. Which article would I submit: the one in favour of Brexit or the one against it? With a faltering hand, I clicked the 'attach files' paperclip, then selected my argument for Remain.

ZZZHUM! There was suddenly a blinding flash of electric-blue light. Blinking, I swivelled my office chair to find a figure standing behind me. He was a man advanced in years, though virile and ruggedly attractive. His face was deeply lined, his blond hair streaked with grey. He wore a patch over his right eye and his outfit suggested some dystopian future (it was leather, with metal bits on it).

'Who the hell are you?' I exclaimed. 'Announce yourself, stranger!'

'I am you,' he replied, 'the Boris Johnson of 2034. I have travelled back in time to meet the Boris of 2016.'

As ridiculous as it sounded, I could not disbelieve him. His visible intelligence, his regal bearing, the bulge in his crotch region: all were eerily familiar. I stood and shook his hand.

'Thrilled to meet my favourite person. To what do I owe this pleasure?'

'I come from a land of smoke and ashes. The seas boil and the skies rain fire and brimstone. Only a thousand humans survive, and all of them envy the dead.'

'Crikey. So climate change really shafts us?'

'It wasn't that. It was you.'

I had been accused of many misdemeanours, but ending the world wasn't one of them. I implored my futuristic visitor to explain.

'In my timeline, you file an article calling for Britain to stay in the EU. This results in a Remain landslide on 23 June. Emboldened by their victory, the Eurocrats go too far. They pass a series of insane laws, banning pints and making our official language Portuguese. When Britain resists, the EU quells dissent by building an army of cyborgs. These become self-aware, turning on their human masters and laying waste to the world.'

'By Jove,' I said. 'How beastly.'

The older Boris nodded.

'I came back to avert this fate.'

'You mean like the Terminator?'

'Yes,' he said, 'exactly like the Terminator.'

'Right . . . I suppose I should tell people to vote Leave.'

'That would be ideal,' he said. 'Oh, and one last tip: when you meet Carrie, use a second SIM card. You don't want Marina reading those texts.'

There came another flash of light and Future Boris was gone. It was like a Hollywood blockbuster, one with a big special effects budget. I turned back to my computer and, shuddering, deleted the pro-Remain article. I submitted the one advocating Leave and the rest, as they say, is history.

So there you have it. No matter how bad the country gets as a result of Brexit, I did absolutely the right thing.

CHAPTER TEN

You Brexit, You Buy It

After an undesired victory,
Boris makes a tilt for the premiership.

Now an out-and-proud Leaver, I threw myself into the maelstrom of the EU referendum. I signed up for the Vote Leave campaign, joining Scottish creep Michael Gove and Northern creep Dominic Cummings (more on him to come). They saw themselves as the brains of the operation, while I was the charismatic frontman. In truth, I was both charismatic and brainy. Nonetheless, I deigned to follow their lead. They would draw up lists of disadvantaged areas and launch me at them like a thermonuclear missile. But a thermonuclear missile that actually helps its target.

The campaign took me to places I never thought I'd go. Specifically, the North of England. Having taken pains to avoid them, I was now giving speeches in towns like Middlesborough, Barnsley and Blyth. The Northerners came out in their thousands, flat caps doffed respectfully, whippets leashed with string.

'Ey up, Boris,' they would say. 'I like tha style. You may have gone t' Eton and that, but you understand us ordinary folk. Folk what was born down coal mine and don't read t'*Guardian*.'

These goodnatured simpletons, later designated 'Red Wall voters', would go on to deliver my landslide in 2019. I treasured my time among them, learning their backward ways and chuckling at their short vowels. By the end of the campaign, I considered myself a spiritual Northman. Though obviously it was a blessed relief to get back to London, where everything's not in black and white and you can buy half-decent focaccia.

It was all fun and games until the vote itself. When it became clear that Leave had edged it, my response was utter panic. I had only intended to scare the establishment, win the hearts and minds of Eurosceptics and put myself in poll position to become the next PM. Now people would expect me to take responsibility for Britain actually leaving. I felt like the protagonists of Mel Brooks's *The Producers*, with Brexit as my 'Springtime for Hitler'. Oh god, oh god, oh god . . .

And so we return to the first scene of this volume: in media res, baby! The referendum results had just been announced – Leave 52 per cent, Remain 48 per cent – and I was flummoxed and flabbergasted, poleaxed and petrified. I stumbled about the room, grabbing underlings by the lapels and howling in their faces: 'Oh shitting fuck! Oh Christing hell! Millions will be ruined! How could you let this happen to me?!'

Once I'd been properly sedated, the upside became apparent. Cameron had staggered out of Number Ten and resigned in humiliation. 'Take that, Cammy,' I thought. 'That's what you get for making me feel bad about my 2:1!' More important than vengeance was the vacancy in the top job. I wanted to be Prime Minister, whether of a prosperous, inclusive nation or an isolated, financial basket case. Now was my time to seize the crown. I would need help, so immediately I called the most loyal and least weird chap I knew: Michael Gove.

At the outset of the 2016 Tory leadership contest, every analyst agreed that I was the frontrunner. It seemed I had a lock on Number Ten, with Remainers in shambles and the Govester firmly in my corner. After all, the competition was comprised of no-hopers like Stephen Crabb, Andrea Leadsom and Theresa May, whose sole personality trait was that she once wore leopard-print heels. These clods would be blown away, leaving the World King to claim his birthright. I was measuring the curtains in the Downing Street boudoir.

Then, just as my campaign was about to launch officially, it happened. Like some WWE wrestler, Michael Gove leapt from the top rope and brought a steel folding chair down on my head. He announced that he was withdrawing his support, claiming: 'Boris cannot provide the leadership or build and unite the team in order to take this country forward.' In addition to being bunk, hokum and poppycock of the first water, this was a vicious act of treachery. Et tu, Michael! It was an instance – sadly not the last – of my loyal friendship being rewarded by dorsal puncture.

Michael's principled objection to my becoming Prime Minister was accompanied by a conviction that he should occupy the role. However, his own campaign soon collapsed. I felt no sense of schadenfreude: my soul was and is too generous for that. I certainly didn't punch the air, then text him 'suck on that, you speccy freak'.

Following Gove's betrayal, I watched in horror as Number Ten fell into the tedious clutches of Theresa May. May was a woman of such nugatory charisma that she made John Major look like Elvis. We had never seen eye to eye, her dour schoolmarm persona clashing with my naughty schoolboy vibe. For these reasons, I anticipated a lengthy stint on the backbenches. I was therefore surprised to be invited to Downing Street as May put together her Cabinet.

I found myself across a desk from the newly minted PM. She made her best attempt at a smile.

'Good news, Boris,' she said, as cold and awkward as ever. 'I want you to be my Foreign Secretary. As you know, it's one of the four Great Offices of State.'

'Foreign Secretary? Splendid! So I'll be in charge of Brexit?'

'No,' quoth May, 'that'll be David Davis at the Department for Exiting the European Union.'

'Ah. But I'll be the point man for tasty new trade deals? Exploiting the myriad opportunities Brexit affords?'

'That's the purview of the Department for International Trade. No, Boris, you'll be tasked with shaking hands, posing for photographs and being out of the country as much as possible.'

I beamed at the robot woman in a pantomime of gratitude. Naturally, I saw through her immediately. May was keeping her friends close and her enemies closer. She believed she could neuter the big dog by giving him a plum assignment. If Boris is bound by Cabinet responsibility, she reasoned, there's a limit to how much mischief he can make.

Oh ho ho, I thought. Good luck with that . . .

CHAPTER ELEVEN

Johnny Foreigner

Boris joins the jet set and sells Global Britain abroad.

As a political rock star, it was only natural that I should go on tour. This is the main perk of being Foreign Secretary – one can hop on a private jet and stamp one's carbon footprint across the globe. Nominally, one does so to advance British interests, bolster relations with allies and shore up national security. In practice, one does it to generate photos of one looking important. I loved playing the role of dignitary, attending countless banquets and wearing turbans, garlands and brightly coloured robes. At such events, I would enchant my hosts with ethnic humour and impressions of their accent. To quote my dude Willy S, 'All the world's a stage.' I cavorted upon that stage, giving encore after encore, until I got the hook.

My underlings at the Foreign Office wanted to avoid sending me to countries where I might not be welcome. Obviously the EU member states were peeved about the whole Brexit thing.

Then there were all the places I had mocked in my books, columns and public appearances. These included China, Russia, most of the Commonwealth and pretty much all of Africa. Where, I wondered, would I be permitted to visit? Antarctica? It was political correctness gone mad. Do we really want to live in a world in which lifelong xenophobia impedes one's career as a diplomat? This was a matter of free speech. People may not agree with my racist jokes, but they should defend to the death my right to make them.

Perhaps the most consequential development during my time as Foreign Secretary was the election of Donald J. Trump as President of the United States. I confess I was initially alarmed at the rise of this boorish real estate tycoon. He made inflammatory statements, turning people against each other. He was a shameless self-publicist with no political convictions. And he had come to national fame by appearing on a dumb TV show. Yet the more I thought about it, the more Trump grew on me. Strangely, I found myself drawn to this corrupt, dishonest demagogue, with his boundless need for attention and his insane blond hairdo.

I resolved to make a success of our relationship. Especially since, post-Brexit, the Yanks could buy and sell our asses. In the end, the pair of us – despite our differences – established an easy rapport. To illustrate, here is a transcript of my first phone call with President-elect Trump.

JOHNSON: First off, enormous congratulations, Donald.

TRUMP: Call me Mr Trump.

JOHNSON: Gosh, yes, my apologies – congratulations, Mr Trump.

TRUMP: Actually, call me Mr President.

JOHNSON: Mr President, of course. May I say how honoured I am to be speaking with you? I'm an *Apprentice* superfan from back in the day, and I've read *The Art of the Deal* five times.

TRUMP: That's five more than I have.

JOHNSON: Well, I'm delighted you won. Everybody in the UK loves you. Not like that dreadful Obama. I actually wrote a column about 'the part-Kenyan President's ancestral dislike of the British empire.'

TRUMP: This is what I've been saying: the guy's from Kenya. And he's a Muslim, which means he can't be President. It's called the White House for a reason, don't you think?

JOHNSON: Ah . . . Well . . . Um . . .

TRUMP: Listen, I like you. I hear people call you the British Trump.

JOHNSON: That's . . . very flattering.

TRUMP: But I'm the American Trump, okay? Which means bigger, better and with hotter women. Don't you forget that.

EXAGGERATED
GESTURES

ILL
FITTING
SUIT

DICROUS
COIFFURE →

UGHY
YSIQUE →

JOHNSON: I wouldn't dream of it.

TRUMP: Good. If you keep kissing my ass, doing what I say at all times and never standing up to me, we'll get along fine.

JOHNSON: Absolutely – I treasure the special relationship between our countries. Speaking of which, I wonder if I could ask a favour . . .

TRUMP: [Inaudible]

JOHNSON: You see, I rather promised that, after Brexit, we would strike these marvellous trade deals. And given the prodigious size of your GDP—

TRUMP: Okay, we're gonna wrap this up. Kanye West is here to see me.

JOHNSON: Mm, yes, Kanye. Naturally that takes precedence. Let's talk soon, Mr President.

TRUMP: Bye, Norris.

As you can see, diplomacy at its finest. Thank goodness we cast off the shackles of the EU, meaning that Britain would never again be under the thumb of a foreign power!

My tenure as Foreign Secretary was made more difficult by a history of provocative statements about world leaders. One such issue was the vulgar limerick I composed about President Erdoğan, the 'wankerer' from Ankara, whom I accused of having carnal knowledge of a goat. This made discussions with my Turkish counterpart rather tricky. What is less well known is that I penned offensive verses on other leaders. Allow me to share a few:

Frau Chancellor, Angela Merkel,
Is terribly easy to irkel.
That Teutonic frump
Will oft get the hump
And cause good old Boris to smirkel.

Macron has a curious yen:
He thinks older women très bien.
When his wife was his teacher,
He'd often beseech her
To give him a caning again.*

He's a tiny bloke, President Putin,
Of that there can be no disputin'.
I might further assert
He looks foolish sans shirt,
But that would be putting the boot in.

---

* It really is confounding that Macron married a woman twenty-four years his senior. Coincidentally, I am twenty-four years older than Carrie, which is the normal way round.

A lad by the name Kim Jong-un
Loves firing missiles for fun.
He gawps at the rockets
While stroking his cock: it's
His one way to get the job done.

Old Trump has a wandering eye
And never sets standards too high.
Though he yearns for Ivanka,
The wig-wearing wanker
Will grab any pussy nearby.

Reading them together, it seems bizarre that no one's approached me to be Poet Laureate.

CHAPTER TWELVE

BoJo Triumphant

*In which May self-immolates, lighting our hero's
path to Downing Street.*

When Theresa May called a snap general election, to be held on 8 June 2017, I was horrified. Not because I believed my party would lose, but because every poll suggested it would win convincingly. This was my ultimate nightmare: to be locked out of power for at least another five years and watch Theresa grimace her way through the job that should have been mine. May's victory seemed assured: after all, the competition was Labour under Jeremy Corbyn. Corbyn was widely reviled, regarded by the entire media – and most of his own MPs – as a bug-eyed, Stalin-loving terrorist. I assumed the electoral map would turn bluer than a Smurf orgy.

And then – miracle of miracles! – everything went tits up for the Tories. Theresa broke down upon first exposure to the voters, like a malfunctioning animatronic Thatcher. At one point, an interviewer asked the naughtiest thing she had ever done, and she said running through fields of wheat as a child. To be fair, I would have struggled to answer that question, given the abundance of possible answers. Telling your Eton mate you'd help him beat up a journalist? Getting sacked from the Shadow Cabinet for lying about your infidelities? Repeatedly making racist and homophobic comments in your articles and novel? These knock wheat fields into a cocked hat.

Theresa simply could not connect with the British public. She was stiffer than me surrounded by nubile researchers. When she tried to exhibit some spark of humanity, the effect was unnerving rather than endearing. Her experience in Downing Street clearly made her miserable (I haven't the faintest idea why). She was a feel-bad PM at a time when the nation needed bucking up. Perhaps by a golden-haired lothario with a penchant for bawdy grandiloquence . . .

As dismal as the campaign had been, the result was worse than I could have hoped for. The Conservatives lost thirteen seats and, with them, our slender majority. Now we needed to form a minority government with the support of Northern Ireland's Democratic Unionist Party (or 'Day Yow Pay'). Corbyn had exceeded expectations, and I was happier than any of his unwashed, pronoun-wielding supporters. May's goose was cooked. The Wicked Witch of Maidenhead was finally melting.

Like Macbeth, I saw a dagger before me. The only question was when to strike . . .

The 2017 election had resulted in a hung parliament – bloody well hung, as far as I was concerned. While May hobbled along as Prime Minister, I waited in the wings to succeed her. But I didn't want to cock things up like I had with Cameron. I needed to seem sensible, statesmanlike, ambitious but not too ambitious. When the time came to shank the leader, I would need a pretext. That pretext was – what else? – Brexit.

May had battled for months to come up with a version of Brexit that would appease headbangers in the parliamentary party without obliterating the economy. She called her Cabinet to the Prime Minister's country house so that we could agree on a strategy. I was all for the resulting 'Chequers plan', leading a toast to it at dinner. Then I learned that David Davis was going to resign in protest. If he did so and I did not, I would look like a cuck, a softie and a big girl's blouse. After an agonising back and forth, I decided to merk my second PM. I announced my resignation, declaring that May's plan 'sticks in the throat'. Of course, what really stuck in my throat was not being Prime Minister.

Alas, my self-detonation did not have the desired effect. May, ever the Remainer, stuck it out in Downing Street. Her premiership was like the eponymous ghouls in *The Walking Dead,* and I, the rugged protagonist, had failed to land a headshot. Returning to the backbenches was dispiriting. Nonetheless, I did everything I could to make life hard for May. I fulminated against her Chequers plan, calling it a fraudulent mess, a constitutional abortion, a slap in the face of Britannia. If I'm honest, she could have struck the best deal imaginable – full access to European markets, with a lifetime's supply of champagne and bratwurst for all British citizens – and I'd still have opposed it.

Theresa was buffeted from every angle, suffering two votes of no confidence and three rejections by Parliament of her withdrawal agreements. It was the prime ministerial version of the Saw franchise: endless scenes of excruciating torture. Finally, blessedly, May gave up the ghost in the month of 2019 that bears her name. Brexit had felled a second Downing Street resident. Boris was back in business!

Before I could be Prime Minister, there was the matter of the Conservative leadership contest. MPs would hold a series of votes, whittling down the list of candidates. The final two would then be voted on by the party membership. A word about the Tory membership: old. Two words: very old. The average Conservative is a nonagenarian homeowner with a burning hatred of Meghan Markle. They tend to favour capital punishment and compulsory golliwog ownership. But they aren't the worst. Have you ever met a Young Conservative? They make too much eye contact, bang on about Ayn Rand and always look inexplicably moist. Anyway, these freaks were all in for BoJo.

Given my popularity among the membership, MPs were my main concern. Truth be told, I had never enjoyed warm relations with the parliamentary party. Sure, they recognised my box office mojo and potency as a campaigner, but their love was conditional. For some strange reason, a great number of Tory MPs viewed me as unserious, untrustworthy, fickle, haphazard, incompetent, intemperate and corrupt. A moral vacuum who had cheated on every woman he had been with and was just as likely to screw over his party and country. Where people get such notions I will never know.

To win over my reticent colleagues, I launched a charm offensive. In political circles, this is known as 'pressing the flesh'. It wasn't the kind of flesh-pressing I typically enjoy, but I was able to lie back and think of Downing Street. I would wine and dine MPs, larding them with thick layers of chumminess. Most politicians just want to feel important, so before each meeting I would bone up on their histories, pet policies and names. I also promised everyone I spoke to a big fat job in my administration. Of course, there weren't enough vacancies, but I would burn that bridge when I came to it.

This manoeuvring bore fruit. Through a mix of flattery, bribery and their own cowardice, dozens of MPs were persuaded to back my bid. The majority still believed I would steer HMS

Britain straight into the iceberg. But they also thought I was best placed to win elections, and so held their noses. I sailed through five rounds of voting, the final two candidates being yours truly and Jeremy 'Freudian slip' Hunt.

Hunt was what passed for a moderate in the modern Conservative party, which meant he preferred austerity to threatening asylum seekers with a blunderbuss. He was also a Remainer, a sin tantamount to bestiality. He spent the ensuing weeks trying to talk some sense into the membership. They didn't listen (perhaps their hearing aids malfunctioned). Meanwhile, I maintained a low profile. As the frontrunner, there was no upside to my appearing before cameras, giving interviews or telling people what I would actually do as Prime Minister. Better to keep that a fun surprise, like drawing a chance card in Monopoly. I replicated this disappearing act in the 2019 general election, to similar success.

When the blue-rinse brigade cast their votes, they were over-whelmingly in favour of Boris. I would now be Leader of the Conservative party (yawn) and thus Prime Minister (yay). I was beside myself, having finally fulfilled my boyhood ambition. Much of the public despaired, but they would come around. What was the worst that could happen?

PART THREE:

BOZ THE GREAT AND TERRIBLE
(2019–present)

CHAPTER THIRTEEN

PM BJ

*Boris enters Downing Street, ushering Britain
into a golden age.*

In my inaugural speech as Prime Minister, I paid tribute to 'the fortitude and patience of my predecessor'. This felt appropriate, given that I had done more than anyone to test those qualities. As I walked through the iconic doors, I made myself a promise. I was going to be a different kind of PM. Not some Gloomy Gus like Theresa May or Gordon Brown, freighted with the awesome responsibility of the role. No, I would lead Britain into the 2020s with ebullience and jeu d'esprit. Boris Johnson was going to have fun.

And so it proved. I revelled in the prestige of my title. Suddenly, everything I touched could be given that sweetest of adjectives, 'prime ministerial'. Here was my prime ministerial desk, my prime ministerial stapler, my prime ministerial tube of Durex Play Lubricant Gel. Then there were the perks. People had been sucking up to me for years, but now the up-sucking intensified. I no longer had yes men, I had yes, yes, yes men, orgasmic in their agreement. Meanwhile, business types fell over themselves to offer me lavish meals, interest-free loans and use of their private jets and holiday homes.

I loved the trappings of the office, from the Number Ten letterhead to weekly meetings with the Queen. Best of all was Chequers, the Prime Minister's grace-and-favour mansion. Located in leafy Buckinghamshire, the estate was gifted to the country in 1917, to provide PMs with a place for rest and recreation. Its previous owner, Sir Arthur Lee, argued that 'the better the health of our rulers, the more sanely will they rule'. I spent as much time as I could at Chequers, hence the notable sanity of my government. I would play the role of country squire, waited on hand and foot by a wonderfully attentive staff. And who picked up the bill? Our good old friend the taxpayer!

My initial stint in Downing Street would see a soupçon of constitutional crisis. Or, as I like to call it, Prorogue One: A Boris Story. Here's what happened – my deadline for Brexit was fast approaching, but a deal with the EU had not been reached. I wanted Britain to leave Noel Edmonds style, which is to say Deal or No Deal. Unfortunately, Remainers were trying to block the latter option, on the basis that it would tank the economy. My brain trust came up with a solution: drop the P-bomb. By getting the Queen to prorogue (or suspend) Parliament, I could prevent it from passing legislation to nix No Deal. There was concern about politicising the Crown, but I thought the idea splendid. I got on the blower to Lizzie and told her to prorogue away.

For some reason, this made a lot of people hopping mad. There were impromptu protests, legal challenges and exhortations to 'stop the coup'. Ultimately the Supreme Court* ruled that I had told the Queen to act unlawfully. HRH was not best pleased, as she made clear by phone call. I'm sure the Palace won't mind my sharing a transcript.

BJ: Gosh, um, Your Majesty. It's wonderful to hear from you. How are you—

ER: Listen, you overfilled wanksock. My advisers say you messed me around on this prorogation shit. We are not fucking amused.

BJ: Ah. Well. I'm – I'm dreadfully sorry to—

ER: 'Ooh, I'm dreadfully sorry, I'm dreadfully sorry.' If you were here now, I'd beat you senseless with my diamond-encrusted phone.

BJ: As your obedient subject, I would gladly take the beating.

---

* Which I thought was an American thing. Turns out we have one – who knew?

89

ER: Blah blah blah. Look, I have enough on my plate dealing with Andrew. If this comes back to bite me on the arse, I'll feed your bollocks to my corgis.

End of call.

I wasn't too worried, though. I knew Liz couldn't stay cross with her roguish proroguer.

During those tumultuous months, I was fortunate to have Carrie by my side. Prime ministers always depend on the counsel and emotional support of their wives and husbands. Ever the innovator, I brought the first prime ministerial girlfriend into Downing Street. Drawing upon American tradition, some have described Carrie as my 'first lady'. Well, she was far from my first lady and I doubt she'll be my last. Just kidding!

The moment I laid eyes on Carrie, I wanted to lay other things on her. A media consultant by trade, she is redoubtable, ambitious, a force of nature. She ascended the party ranks with astonishing rapidity, despite accusations of absenteeism and bogus expense claims. She is a woman of many passions, from going on holiday to interior design to . . . I dunno, animals or something. Also, Carrie is much younger than me, which – among other advantages – gives me insight into the millennial world-view.

Like that paragon of good taste Alan Partridge, Carrie's

favourite band is ABBA. The palindromic Swedish quartet provided a soundtrack to our courtship and subsequent marriage. She offered to lay all her love on me, and I said gimme, gimme, gimme. She was my dancing queen, I her super trouper. While some warned she was after my money, money, money, I still took a chance on her. Our relationship is yet to meet its Waterloo, and if that isn't a fairy tale, then my name's Fernando. Mamma Mia! Also, Carrie thinks it terribly cool that I was a teenager when ABBA released their hits (she wasn't yet born).

At this juncture, I should like to engage head-on with some vile distortions about our relationship. Firstly, it has been reported that the MP Conor Burns walked into my Commons office to find us in a 'compromising situation'. Specifically, BJ getting a BJ. Such prurience is typical of the press. Can't a man leave his wife of twenty-five years for a younger woman without them turning it into something sleazy? There is nothing tawdry in how Carrie and I got together. It was the classic love story: boy meets girl, boy spends a lot of time alone with girl, boy tries to hire girl as boy's Chief of Staff. Except, instead of being a boy, I was a married Foreign Secretary.

Secondly, there was that nonsense about a fight. In the final stages of the 2019 Conservative leadership election, police were called to our Camberwell flat after an 'altercation involving screaming, shouting and banging'. Apparently our neighbours imagined some kind of Punch and Judy scenario. In reality,

Carrie was playing her *ABBA Gold* CD at high volume, which meant we had to raise our voices.

'I LOVE YOU, BORIS!' she screamed. 'I COULD NOT WISH FOR A MORE FAITHFUL OR CONSIDERATE PARTNER!'

'I WILL ALWAYS TREAT YOU WITH KINDNESS AND RESPECT!' I bellowed back.

Then we began discussing our future wedding. I suggested, given my famous love of the classical world, that it could be Greek-themed. To illustrate Hellenic customs, I smashed a succession of plates and glasses. If our neighbours thought something untoward was happening, then that only displays the depths of their ignorance.

Finally, it has been argued that, in Downing Street, Carrie would exercise undue influence on my decision-making. As a former comms officer, Carrie has a healthy interest in politics and naturally made her views known on policies, personnel and so forth. Yes, she would send me hundreds of WhatsApps during top-level meetings, and yes, I would tell advisers I had to appease 'er indoors. But the idea she pulled my strings is for the birds. People talk as though I were henpecked, with Carrie forever brandishing her rolling pin. This is deeply sexist, something I would never be.

A girlfriend was not my only addition to the Downing Street flat. Soon after I entered office, Carrie and I were joined by Dilyn, a rescue dog. While Carrie loved having more content

93

for her Instagram, I regarded the mutt with a jaundiced eye. I've never been the nurturing type – just ask my kids – and Dilyn required constant attention. He wasn't housetrained, so would gambol through the corridors of power, defecating, micturating and chewing on priceless books and furniture. My patience soon wore thin. People say that pets resemble their owners, but Dilyn and I had nothing in common. He was an oblivious beast who made a mess and expected those around him to clean it up. He was sexually incontinent, humping anything that moved. Worst of all, he defiled the Prime Minister's office. Try as I might, I could not empathise.

By October 2019 I realised that my position at Number Ten was untenable. Cold Fish May had left me with a useless turd of a Parliament. Is there such a thing as a useful turd? Manure, I suppose. The point is, I didn't have sufficient MPs to approve my Brexit withdrawal agreement. It was therefore imperative that I change the parliamentary maths. The only way to do this was to call a general election. I worried I might lose and become the shortest-lived Prime Minister in history (shout-out to Liz Truss). On the other hand, Jeremy Corbyn was getting slated by every paper to the right of the *Morning Star*, so I fancied my chances. I bit the bullet and fired the starting pistol.

My campaign boffins devised a lapidary slogan: Get Brexit Done. I was instructed to repeat these words at every possible opportunity, regardless of context, until they lost all meaning. Whatever the question, 'get Brexit done' would be my answer. *Par exemple*:

'How will you address the crisis in NHS waiting times?'

'To deal with the backlog, we need to get Brexit done.'

'Are minorities right to be offended by your comments?'

'What those communities really care about is getting Brexit done.'

'Would you like fries with that?'

'Get Brexit done.'

'What will be your priorities once you've got Brexit done?'

'To get Brexit done.'

'Mr Johnson, do y—'

'Get Brexit done, get Brexit done, get Brexit done.'

Soon I was burbling those four syllables in my sleep. It seeped getbrexitdone into my subconscious getbrexitdone and haunted my getbrexitdone dreams. It was the prescription for all Britain's ailments: a miracle drug called Gebrexidone.

My chief tactic was to avoid any scrutiny. It was expected that I would submit to a grilling by ruddy Scotsman Andrew Neil, a man who loves the sound of his own voice even more than I do. With Machiavellian aplomb, I allowed Corbyn to go on Neil's show and receive a fire-alarm bollocking, then declined to go on myself. The Brillo-headed interrogator was enraged. BoJo: 10, BBC: Nil. On other occasions, I dodged questions by pocketing a reporter's phone and hiding in a fridge. For such hijinks I was lambasted on social media and in the broadsheets. Even *Have I Got News for You* had a go, the ingrates.

But guess what: none of it mattered. Come 12 December, I was victorious, with a stonking eighty seat majority! The British people had sent a clear message: they wanted to get Brexit done. What's more, they had entrusted their futures and those of their families to Boris Johnson. The absolute rubes . . .

CHAPTER FOURTEEN

World King at Last

And when Boris saw the breadth of his domain,
he wept, for there were no more worlds to conquer.

Going into Christmas 2019, it's fair to say BoJo was on top of the world. Comrade Corbyn had been packed off home to Leningrad. The parliamentary party stood behind me, its ranks swelled by moronic Red Wallers who couldn't believe their luck. Five long years of power lay ahead, if not ten, fifteen or twenty. With a personal mandate from the voting public, I had the means to transform the state in any way I saw fit. Finally I could forge ahead with the policies I really cared about, such as . . . I'll get back to you on that. The point is, I won. I was poised to fulfil my lifelong dream: joining the pantheon of great prime ministers. It would take a colossal oaf to fumble such an opportunity.

Before remaking Britain, though, I was in dire need of a vacay. Carrie and I beetled off to the private island of Mustique, in which tropical paradise we spent a rejuvenating ten days. We stayed at a luxury Moroccan-style stone villa, with six double bedrooms, three private swimming pools, two bars, a library and four dedicated staff: a butler, chef, gardener and house-keeper. Predictably, there was much grumbling when it emerged that our holiday had been paid for by a millionaire Conservative donor. This, I'm afraid, is no more than the politics of envy. What is wrong with the founder of Carphone Warehouse doing a favour for his mate, the serving PM, out of pure generosity? The idea that this might constitute some form of corruption is doolally. Do people really believe that Boris Johnson's political judgement can be swayed by white sand beaches and azure seas? Ooh, and those fancy cocktails with the little umbrellas in them . . .

Unfortunately, being Prime Minister is not a one-man show. You can't just catapult around the country, making speeches and promising money for projects that never materialise. Instead, you must seek to govern through Cabinet. Not the fun kind of cabinet, stocked with Bombay Sapphire and Macallan 21. No, the kind filled with grasping weirdos who would stab you in the back as soon as look at you.

Following my triumph in the 2019 election, I decided a reshuffle was in order. This new Cabinet was never going to be made up of world-beaters. I had turfed out my non-loony colleagues during the Brexit Wars, and now our side of the

Commons looked like Arkham Asylum. I therefore chose to surround myself with rank mediocrities, the kind of clueless chair-fillers that could never hope to challenge me.

As Chancellor I installed Rishi Sunak, a diminutive plutocrat who didn't know how to use a debit card. Foreign Secretary was Dominic Raab, a man likely to be found shirtless, punching holes in the office wall and screaming, 'Do you want some?' Home Secretary was Priti Patel, a smirking sadist. Matt 'Cringe in Human Form' Hancock remained at the Department for Health, where I hoped he wouldn't be tested by any kind of emergency. I allowed Gove the preposterous title 'Chancellor of the Duchy of Lancaster', reasoning that he had already betrayed me once and was unlikely to do so again. Also in the mix were Liz Truss and Kwasi Kwarteng: both barmy, but harmless as long as they were kept away from the levers of power.

Having created this team of losers, I was obliged, regrettably, to spend time with them. Cabinet meets once a week, in the pro-saically named Cabinet Room, for a veritable orgy of boredom. One sits at a long table as each minister bangs on about their bailiwick. Here's Rishi's tight five on interest rates. Now Ben Wallace wants to talk defence spending. I would do my best to liven things up with gags, anecdotes and impersonations of various ethnic groups. But it seemed I had picked a Cabinet of humourless dolts. They were never in the mood for The BoJo Show, preferring to focus on such mundane drivel as hospital waiting times and the economy. Being forced to listen to them caused me acute psychic pain. If I'm in a room and someone else is talking, things have gone horribly wrong.

Aside from that unpleasantness, everything was hunky dory. I stood at the peak of my powers, like Sonic the Hedgehog when he collects all six chaos emeralds and turns into Super Sonic. On 31 January 2020, Britain officially left the EU, a momentous occasion I celebrated by banging a little gong. The gong broke, which I chose not to see as an omen. I was jubilant, drunk on possibility (and also alcohol). We had got Brexit done! Now the impasse was over, we could shower Britain with the rewards of freedom. We would have to work out what those were, exactly. But I was confident that they existed and would delight everyone.

From my vantage point, I saw the future clearly. I would be hailed as the greatest Conservative Prime Minister of all time, like if Winston Churchill and Margaret Thatcher had a baby (apologies for the mental image). Free of the yoke of Brussels, Britannia would surge forth, her coffers full to bursting. Crime and unemployment would plummet to zero per cent. The NHS would bounce back from years of underfunding, stronger than ever. The North would be revitalised by my levelling-up agenda, which wouldn't cost any money or piss off Tories down South. Bold infrastructure projects would spring up across the land: a bridge between Scotland and Northern Ireland and an escalator to the moon. I had no doubt that 2020 would be the best year ever.

Barring, of course, some global catastrophe . . .

CHAPTER FIFTEEN

Veni Covidi Vici

A viral sensation comes straight outta Wuhan.

Just my luck. I win a landslide election, settle the matter of Brexit, and what do I get hit with? The worst public health crisis since 1918, when Spanish flu caused millions of permanent siestas. It was a boot aimed squarely at the Johnson gonads.

When I first heard of a virus spreading in China, I thought 'no biggie'. Let the eggheads sort it out, while I focus on more important things, like writing my Shakespeare book. I saw no need to engage with the twin acronyms of SAGE and COBRA. Instead, I left Covid in the capable hands of Matt Hancock (if you've seen the footage, you know what those hands are capable of). The disease may have been ravaging far-off places like South Korea and Italy, but the United Kingdom felt safe. No doubt its virions would turn back from our shores, dazzled by the white cliffs of Dover.

Suddenly the scientists changed their tune. One moment they

were bullish about controlling the coronavirus. The next they were declaring it an unstoppable wave. I was advised to pursue a strategy of herd immunity. Having always seen the British as bovine, this appealed to me. We would let Covid rip through the population, then get on with our lives. Most of us, anyway. The virus had other ideas. New modelling showed the health service would be inundated and face collapse. Desperate times called for desperate measures – I didn't want the egg of mass death on my face.

The notion of curtailing people's rights made me deeply uncomfortable. I am by nature a libertarian (and, indeed, a libertine). I prize freedom above all: freedom of speech, freedom of assembly, the freedom to cheat on one's wife. Live and let live, I say. In the words of occult sex-freak Aleister Crowley, 'Do what thou wilt shall be the whole law.' Nevertheless, the figures were terrifying. My party's cuts had rendered the NHS a tottering Jenga tower. I would be damned if I was the Prime Minister on whose watch it collapsed.

And so, on 23 March, I found myself staring into a camera, announcing a national lockdown. I had been told to convey gravitas, so with every sinew I fought the urge to pull faces and make quips. Summoning all my willpower, I refrained from saying 'Wuhan, thank you ma'am' or 'If you find yourself coughin', go buy a coffin'. Instead, I solemnly intoned that Britons would have to remain in their homes, only leaving for vital supplies, exercise once a day, medical emergencies and essential work. It felt strange to be imposing rules when I had spent my entire life breaking them. But hey, do as I say, not as I do, right?

I found the new Covid reality a nightmare. Not because tens of thousands of my countrymen were dying, but because it cramped my style. No longer could I socialise with the elite or show off in front of packed audiences. Instead, I was forced to hunker down in Number Ten, gawping at charts and statistics. One can scarcely imagine the tedium of being briefed, day in and day out, by science nerds Patrick Vallance and Chris Whitty. I was a hapless crouton, submerged in a soup of jargon: 'zoonotic', 'flattening the curve', 'the R rate'. Respiratory illness seemed less of a danger than being bored to death. To while away these longueurs, I would jot down poems in my notepad. For instance:

> Amour in the time of Corona
> Can greatly inhibit one's boner.
> To manage the task
> While wearing a mask,
> One practically needs a diploma.

Or:

Pat Vallance and Christopher Whitty
Can sometimes become rather snitty.
They frequently mention
My lack of attention.
Alas, I must tell them 'tough titty'.

Worse than the virus geeks was Matt Hancock, a man who would be out of his depth in a puddle. When Covid kicked off, I naturally wanted to replace him as Health Secretary. Anyone would have been better: Sajid Javid, Olly Murs, a Tamagotchi. However, I needed a fall guy for my government's pandemic response. With his unconvincing smile and big wet eyes, Matt had 'fall guy' written all over him. And so I endured the company of this gauche muppet, this man-sized baby, this alien trying to impersonate a human and failing. It was a constant struggle not to give him a noogie, swirly or atomic wedgie.

Day upon day my cabin fever increased. On the occasions I was allowed out, I did my best to reassure the public that life would go on. I might, say, visit a hospital, shake hands with everybody there, then boast about it. Some colleagues fretted about me contracting a potentially fatal disease. I had no such concerns. Having led a life pleasingly free of consequences, I was sure that all would be well.

*

I awoke on the morning of 26 March feeling rather worse for wear. It was not unlike the hangover one might theoretically experience after an all-night rager at Evgeny Lebedev's Italian castle. But rather than sharing a vodka luge with Katie Price, I had been tucked up at a respectable hour. Now my head was pounding and my limbs ached. It was like I had gone ten rounds with a bulldozer. Still, I flung myself out of bed, rolled across to the prime ministerial bathroom and crammed myself in the shower. I had important business to conduct: places to go, people to see, faces to breathe in.

I strode into the office, doing my best to exude strength and dignity.

'Up and at 'em! Allons-y! Hands off your cocks and on with your socks!'

One of my comely aides rose to greet me.

'Good morning, sir. Is . . . Is everything all right?'

'Mmm, yes, absolutely. I'm pumped and raring to go. Another day of levelling up, smashing trade deals and delivering for the British peo—'

Here I collapsed into a paroxysm of wheezing and spluttering. Members of my staff endeavoured subtly to back out of the room or lean out the window. The aforementioned aide stayed put, pulling her blouse over her mouth and nose.

'Prime Minister, you don't look well. You've gone the colour of soured cream and you're sweating like Niagara Falls. The carpet's soaked.'

'I've no idea what you're talking about. I never felt better in my life.'

'Right ... It's just you're currently on the floor, in foetal position, shaking violently.'

'Nothing that a splash of coffee won't fix.'

I was raised to see illness as a form of moral weakness: one should always soldier on, in spite of one's shattered pelvis or acute radiation poisoning. My aide pursued her line of enquiry.

'Do you think you might have Covid?'

'Don't be ridiculous. I've followed every guideline to the lett—'

I broke off to expectorate for about ten minutes.

The next day a Covid test confirmed that I was afflicted, infected and pozzed up to the max. It made no sense: how could my mighty constitution fail me? After all, my body was a temple. A temple of Dionysus, perhaps, but a temple nonetheless. I resolved to battle on. My government's instructions were to isolate, but isolation and Boris make unhappy bedfellows. Too much time on my own and I start having morbid thoughts. For this reason, I ordered a succession of special advisers to come and see me. I was determined to keep working in the throes of Covid. I don't remember that period too clearly, but I fear my decision-making may have been impaired. Glancing over my correspondence, I find the following memos:

- Dom, can we make a city that goes all bendy like Inception? Look into it.
- Important question: if a penguin could fly, would he be made king of the penguins, or shunned/killed?
- Do people love me really or asfahidgoeitneaginaocmkae-pihghaniweeeeee

For the first time in my premiership, I was distracted, incoherent, checked out. After a certain point, I sat at my keyboard, typing the same sentence over and over: All Covid and no crowds makes Boris a dull boy.

On 5 April, my condition became dramatically worse, and my retinue insisted that I go to hospital. Wheezing like Darth Vader with his mask off, I said not on their nelly. I was well aware that, in the event of my incapacitation, Dominic Raab would become Acting Prime Minister. Dominic 'Begbie' Raab is a clench-jawed psycho with veins popping up all over his brow. Worse still, the guy has a black belt in karate. If he managed to get behind my desk, we would have a hell of a job getting him back out. I could order my Personal Protection Officers to help, but what if he immobilised them with a series of chops, throws and roundhouse kicks? Ultimately these concerns were moot: my staff bundled me off to Guy's and St Thomas' hospital.

I was somewhat trepidatious, given what my party had been

doing to the NHS for the previous decade, but the quality of care I received was outstanding. The team of doctors and nurses worked tirelessly to stabilise me, to make me comfortable and to reassure me in my hour of need. I found myself wishing they were paid a fair wage. Then I remembered all the donors who needed tax cuts and thought better of it. Despite the Herculean efforts of these brave men and women, my health continued to deteriorate.

The 6 April saw me struggling to breathe, so I was given emergency oxygen and taken to the intensive care unit. Lying there, I entered a state of delirium. Suddenly I was floating up to the ceiling and gazing down at my stricken form. Of course I had read about 'out of body experiences', but I had no idea it would feel so liberating. I was now just a soul: incorporeal, able to do whatever I liked. I found I could pass through walls and considered a look at the women's changing room. Then, without wishing to do so, I floated up again, out of the hospital and into the skies above London. Below me I could see the Palace of Westminster, the mighty Thames, and a bunch of the eyesores I signed off on as mayor.

I kept drifting up and up, until my spirit danced among the stars. It was at this point that things started to get weird. I entered a kaleidoscopic tunnel of light, allowing me to traverse the bounds of space and time. I saw the Blitz, the Battle of Hastings, the original performance of *Hamlet*, with Shakespeare himself as the Ghost. I witnessed my own conception, which, to be honest, I could have done without.

Finally, I found myself in some kind of liminal space, one which defied the laws of geometry. Its walls were crystalline and pulsed with a strange power. Before me stood an old man, robed in white, his expression kindly. He looked a little like my father, Stanley, but gave off less creepy vibes.

'Hello Boris,' he said. 'Welcome to the astral plane.'

'If this is a plane, I'd better be in first class.'

Even as a disembodied spirit, I was still very funny.

'That's very funny,' said the senex.

'Quite so, old boy. Now, give me the skinny: Am I dead?'

'You are neither alive nor dead. I have brought you to this realm to receive the wisdom of ages.'

With that, the snow-haired coot vanished and was replaced by a trio of spirits. One of them stepped forward. I recognised him instantly from his baby face, ovoid physique and smouldering cigar.

'My God,' I exclaimed. 'Winston Churchill!'

'Boris,' rumbled the great man, 'you have always venerated me. But you are more heroic than I.'

'Gosh,' I said. 'Well, if that's what you believe, who am I to contradict you?'

A second figure stepped forth. This one was small, slender, with round glasses and a grey moustache. He spoke in a soft, Indian voice.

'Britain is lucky to have a wise and holy man as Prime Minister. I wish I had offered my people such leadership.'

'Much obliged, Gandhi.'

I turned to the last of the three, a bearded bloke with long, dark hair, a crown of thorns, and holes in each of his upturned palms.

'Who the devil are you?'

'I am Jesus of Nazareth. I just wanted to say, I'm a huge fan. And so's my dad.'

'Splendid, splendid.'

I turned from the group, paused, then turned back.

'While I have you all here . . . Is there anything I could do to be a better man, or a better Prime Minister?'

'No,' they replied as one. 'You're doing marvellously.'

'So to be 100 per cent clear, I should keep on behaving the way I have, with zero changes?'

'Yes,' responded Churchill, Gandhi and Christ.

The old man in white stood before me once more.

'Boris, it is time you return to the land of the living. Britain – nay, the world – needs a leader. Also, you have a shit-ton of kids to look after.'

With that, the chamber shattered and I plunged back to Earth.

I awoke to find an anxious aide leaning over me.

'Prime Minister, how are you feeling?'

'Better than ever,' I said. 'Now, fetch me a phone and tell the Karate Kid to stand down!'

So there it is: my near-death experience. A brush with the Grim Reaper might have changed a lesser man. Not Boris. I was more the same than ever.

Combatting coronavirus was nothing compared to my next ordeal. A couple of weeks after leaving hospital, I became a father for the fifth time. Well, sixth. Maybe seventh – who's to say? The point is, I had yet another sprog. Carrie demanded I do my bit, mucking in and changing nappies. This struck me as unreasonable, given I was Prime Minister. I didn't have time for heaps of shit: I needed to meet with Gavin Williamson and Suella Braverman. Still, I obeyed, dodging jets from my son's dinky spout.

Then there were the sleepless nights, which added to my post-viral brain fog. I stumbled around the Downing Street office, as forgetful as the souls who drank from the River Lethe. Due to Carrie's desire for a baby and my own aversion to condoms, I was totally exhausted. At the height of a pandemic, the Prime Minister was incapable of doing his job. This would have been true anyway, but now I had sick on my shirts.

CHAPTER SIXTEEN

Cummings and Goings

In which our hero is most horribly betrayed.

Any prime minister, no matter how brilliant, will have gaps in their knowledge, lacunae in their expertise. For me, these included domestic policy, foreign policy, the economy, health, education, the Union, crime, culture and trade. As I prepared to enter Downing Street, it became clear I would need someone to handle all that. Someone who could free me from tedious policy crap and let me focus on my strengths: making jokes and having funny hair. Hence the fateful decision to bring in Dominic Cummings as my Chief Adviser.

I first got to know Cummings on the Vote Leave campaign. I was immediately impressed with the soft-spoken Geordie: he had the name of a porn star – if not the mesomorphic physique – and his hairless noggin was jam-packed with ideas. Allow yourself to be cornered by him and he would rant and rave, sometimes for hours, about innovation and the need to disrupt the civil service. He had all these grand schemes for reform, from paying nurses in crypto to establishing what he called 'NASA for cycle lanes'. While I was a newcomer to the Brexit cause, he was a true believer. He saw Brussels as the Death Star and himself as the intrepid X-Wing about to shove a proton torpedo up its exhaust port.

Dom was also, it must be said, a card-carrying mentalist. His high-end brainboxery came hand in hand with a total contempt for others. If anyone questioned his plans, he would denounce them as idiots, numbskulls and useless f-ing c-s. He thought himself a colossus among garden gnomes: the rest of the world was hidebound, complacent and weak. In retrospect, I should probably have realised he would one day decide that I was a useless f-ing c. Dom's Achilles' heel is his personality. Which, to be fair, is a pretty big heel.

Then there were his clothes. People call me scruffy, but I have nothing on Dom's all-out sartorial assault. He would slouch around the Downing Street office in Crocs, tracksuit bottoms, a half-untucked shirt, a coffee-stained beanie and two scarves. His slovenly style was a form of power dressing: 'Imagine how important I must be to get away with this!' While lesser mortals primped and preened, Dom would shuffle into meetings unshaven, looking like he had spent the previous night in a hedge. As a fellow disdainer of rules – grooming, Covid, basic morality – I respected it. I considered trying to out-scruff him, but feared this might lead to an arms race. After a few days, we would both be wearing bedsheets with holes cut in them and tea cosies on our heads.

Still, we had made a good team on Vote Leave. He could apply his bulging brow to the data while Boris worked the adoring crowd, chucking red meat to the Red Wall. Basically, I was the scantily dressed pop star and Dom was the middle-aged Swedish bloke who wrote all her songs. I thought this dynamic could be replicated in Downing Street. I needed governmental knowhow and more policies than 'be Prime Minister'. He needed someone less unsettling to put forward his ideas. And so this flaxen-haired frog invited the scorpion to clamber aboard.

Dom's present antipathy is surprising when one considers all I did for him. I pumped nitrous oxide into the engine of his Vote Leave campaign, pushing it across the finishing line. I elevated him to become the most potent adviser in Downing Street history – without me, he would have been making YouTube videos about the Common Fisheries Policy. What's more, I gave him support and protection at his lowest point. Gather round, boys and girls, for a tale I call 'Cummings Comes A Cropper: The Bastard of Barnard Castle'.

As far as I am concerned, there is never a good reason to visit the North East. Nonetheless, at the height of the first lockdown, Dom did just that. With his wife exhibiting Covid symptoms, he

packed his family in the car and drove 264 miles to his native Durham. Once the Cummingses had recovered, he felt able to return to London. But he didn't go straight back. Instead, he drove to nearby Barnard Castle to – as he claims – test his eyesight. I cannot say I was familiar with this practice. When one goes to Specsavers, one identifies letters of diminishing size. Dom apparently needs a market town to squint at.

Cummings's actions may strike some as reckless and selfish, a mockery of the sacrifice we asked the public to make. I can't say that bothers me. What did bother me was when *The Guardian* and the *Daily Mirror* reported on his trip. This caused a Category 5 shitstorm. Dom's unprepossessing visage was on the front page of every paper. All across the country, people were baying for his blood. My reputation, never pristine, took a battering.

It was clear I had a tough call to make. Should I dump the guy who ran my whole operation? Or should I defend the most hated man in Britain? As with every major decision, I took it to Dominic Cummings. Funnily enough, he was emphatic that he should stay.

'But Dom,' I said, 'what about the public outcry?'

He clenched his fist, eyes bulging like an anime villain.

'Puny humans! I shall address the media directly. They cannot withstand my intellect.'

I had reservations, but kept them to myself. A press conference was duly held in the Downing Street rose garden. Dom set out his case to the British public, using all the charm he could muster. This made things much, much worse.

The Cummings affair saw support for the Conservative party decline. It also undermined government messaging. As a result, people were less likely to heed regulations during a deadly pandemic. Powerful voices – including many Tory MPs – called for Dom's resignation or sacking. In spite of this, I stood by my man. I acted out of loyalty, camaraderie, a belief in second chances. Also, the guy was doing 90 per cent of my work.

So where did it all go wrong? I won't say Dom went mad with power. He was mad before he had power and still is without it. But he didn't get saner during his time at Number Ten. He would go about calling himself 'de facto Prime Minister', quite forgetting that I know Latin. Whenever I objected to one of his schemes, he suggested I go and paint a model bus. What sealed his fate, though, was butting heads with Carrie.

'Boris,' she would tell me, 'you can't have this unelected, unaccountable figure making decisions behind the scenes. That's my job.'

It hurts when one's work husband clashes with one's wife wife. Both Dom and Carrie were essential to my premiership, to my very sense of self. At the end of the day, though, only one of them has sex with me. Cummings had to go.

Sacking a close colleague is never a pleasant experience, and I am one who abhors interpersonal conflict. However, a true leader must take responsibility for his decisions.

'I'm sorry, old bean,' I said. 'I wish I didn't have to do this. It's Carrie, you see. I don't have a choice.'

I expected Dom to take his dismissal with grace. After all, he'd had a good innings: taken us out of Europe, fired a bunch of people, sent a lot of WhatsApps to Laura Kuenssberg. Instead, his features darkened and his eyes blazed.

'Borisssss,' he hissed. 'I swear upon everything unholy that you will pay for this. I shall henceforth devote myself entirely to your destruction. I shall thwart, block and humiliate you at every stage. Then I shall draw upon eldritch magick to annihilate your bloodline. Yes, I'll get you, and your little dog too!'

'Sleep on it, pal,' I replied. 'I'm sure you'll feel better in the morning.'

Unfortunately, Dom didn't feel better. Instead, he began to wage a deranged vendetta against me. Another prominent Johnson, US president Lyndon Baines,* once said it was 'better to have your enemies inside the tent pissing out, than outside the tent pissing in'. After the Cummings sacking, my tent was

---

* Some historical trivia for you: LBJ had a prodigiously large penis. He was proud of the appendage, calling it 'Jumbo' and regularly showing it off. So the surname isn't all we have in common.

121

engulfed by a towering typhoon of piss, then swept into a sea of shit. Dom was leaking morning, noon and night, the political equivalent of Deepwater Horizon. He would seize my dirty laundry, hold it above his head and shine a laser pointer at the stains. He even started a Substack. Clearly, he felt a duty to warn the public about my dangerous incompetence, but only if they paid £10 a month.

It is a curious quirk of my career that so many colleagues have turned on me. It's almost as though I attract snakes and backstabbers. I suppose I just have bad luck. No need to give it deeper thought.

CHAPTER SEVENTEEN

Lulu Hullabaloo

Much ado about Lytle.

During my reign, there were innumerable attempts to confect scandals where no scandal existed. A legion of detractors would poke holes in my every statement, find fault in the most innocuous of actions. You name the cardinal sin, I was falsely accused of it, from embezzlement to serial arson. The pinkos at *The Guardian* even suggested I was the Zodiac Killer. But of all the made-up controversies, one took the proverbial custard cream. This was the Case of Lulu Lytle and the Golden Wallpaper.

For context: prime ministers have traditionally lived in an apartment above Number Ten. However, Tony Blair moved his family to the larger apartment above Number Eleven, a practice that goes on to this day. When Carrie and I took up residence, we found the flat in a wholly unacceptable state. What Theresa May had done was nothing less than a disgrace. Perhaps you are picturing a scene of dissolution, with syringes scattered about and excrement up the walls. It was worse than that. May had decorated the place with items from the upmarket department store John Lewis. This was the stuff of nightmares.

Perhaps I could, with difficulty, have endured the aesthetic assault. Carrie, on the other hand, was beside herself. She rent her garments and howled obscenities. As a loving partner – as a fellow human – I was compelled to promise a full refurbishment. But how could I afford it? I was a mere Prime Minister, struggling to make ends meet. Sure, the taxpayer provided an annual allowance to furnish my residence, but this was a pitiful thirty grand. I had no choice but to seek assistance from a Tory donor, Lord Brownlow. With his help, we engaged the services of interior decorator Lulu Lytle (who costs a Lulu Lottle).

The usual suspects carped and cavilled. As with the Mustique trip, an act of charity was spun into something sinister: a shabby collusion between the head of government and moneyed interests. Wallpapergate was used to depict me and 'Carrie Antoinette' as out-of-touch elitists. But I ask you: is £112,549 really so much, when the alternative is being consigned to a greige, soul-sucking hellhole? Do critics believe I should content myself with living in a bin? Was I genuinely expected to perform at the highest level without £2,000worth of gold wallpaper? I rest my case.

*

The refurb illustrates an issue I faced throughout my premiership. Namely, how to survive on the parsimonious prime ministerial salary of £164,080. That might sound like a lot to ordinary people: binmen, say, or dirt-eaters. But for someone with my background, it was a pittance. I had become accustomed to a certain lifestyle: bottles of Bollinger, lobsters and ortolan, luxury trips to faraway climes. On top of this, I was dealing with a costly divorce (through no fault of my own) and had to fund numerous progeny. It all adds up.

When impecunious in the past, I could simply take on extra work. Few minded if I half-arsed being an MP or a mayor. As PM it was different: attempts to make a few bob on the side were frowned upon. By and large, I treated my poverty with forbearance. I tightened my belt (not literally) and shopped at budget outlets like Marks & Spencer and Waitrose. Still, I was going through my own cost of living crisis: who could blame me if I accepted a few bungs and took out a few loans? Don't the haters realise how much earning potential I had? What a sacrifice I was making, just to be the most important man in the country?

Whenever some scandal percolated, I would receive a moralistic hectoring at Prime Minister's Questions. These were delivered by Corbyn's successor as Labour leader, Sir Keir Starmer. Sir Keir was a former lawyer with the personality of a wet wipe.

Not having any actual policies, he sought to position himself as a paragon of morality.

'Mr Speaker,' he would drone, 'will the Prime Minister accept that he has been a bad little boy and should apologise to the whole school?'

How I hated his pious perma-wince, his finicky hairdo and his whining voice. He was precisely the sort of dullard I did my best to avoid at Oxford. It was a wonder he could sit on the front bench, given the ten-foot stick up his arse.

To be fair, there is one thing I respect about Starmer: his slipperiness. He changes position more often than a porn star. One day he's for nationalisation of key industries, the next it's a pipe dream. One day Jeremy Corbyn is a good friend who was maligned by the press, the next he's a vicious antisemite with no place in the party. In a sense, Starmer and I are kindred spirits. I took Britain out of the EU by promising an additional £350 million a week for the NHS. He told the Labour membership that he was a socialist, then jettisoned all of his pledges. Game, as they say, recognise game.

CHAPTER EIGHTEEN

The Guilty Parties

P-A-R-T-why? Because I gotta!

Okay, time to set the record straight. My lawyers pleaded with me to avoid this topic, but I feel I have no choice. I must address the crisis that did more to derail my premiership than anything else. Except possibly me. Folks, let's talk about Partygate.

On 30 November 2021, the *Mirror*'s Pippa Crerar reported that a series of parties had taken place in Downing Street in the run-up to Christmas 2020. During this period, London was under restrictions that prohibited gatherings of more than six people. When I became aware of the allegations, I snapped into action. My strategy was simple: deny, deny, deny. Under questioning from Sir Sneer Harder, I declared to the House of Commons that 'all guidance was followed completely in Number Ten'. I had played my hand to perfection. Assuming no evidence got out.

On 7 December, ITV News aired a video of my then-Press

Secretary, Allegra Stratton, yukking it up about a party in Downing Street. The next day I spoke to the Commons, expressing my righteous fury and vowing to get to the bottom of things. Like Claude Rains in *Casablanca*, I was shocked, shocked to find parties going on. The general public were enraged. It seemed that those who made the rules did not feel obliged to follow them. Pissed-up politicos were getting their rocks off while ordinary people missed Mum's funeral.

And then there was the real victim: me. Amid the endless negative coverage, my approval ratings took a nosedive. For the very first time, people looked at Boris Johnson and thought 'liar', 'hypocrite', 'duplicitous worm'. Things became intolerable as more Saturnalia were reported. It was the scandal that refused to die, with new revelations dropping each week. An investigation by the civil servant Sue Gray turned up a series of awkward photos, including yours truly at a birthday gathering, can of Estrella in hand. Even worse, the Metropolitan Police issued fixed penalty notices to me, Rishi Sunak and my then-wife Carrie. Who still is my wife, to be fair to her.

Looking back, Partygate was a storm in a teacup (or rather, a can of Estrella). It was another fatuous furore, cooked up by those who cannot stand the thought of a prime minister having fun. These people – Remainiacs, wokesters, lefty journos – tried to bring me down over something trivial. The outrage they purported to feel was naught but a deluge of crocodile tears.

128

Were Starmer and his ilk genuinely bothered by the rumours? If anything, they should have been impressed: months after a near-death experience, I was back on my feet and partying. Allegedly.

Let me be abundantly clear: these parties never happened. The suggestion that Downing Street staff were 'having it large' while the British public made sacrifices is false, slanderous and shameful. It makes a mockery of the valiant efforts of my team during a gruelling and unprecedented period. For this reason, I shall repeat myself: these parties never happened.

But if they did, here's how they would have gone . . .

The clock shows 4.59 p.m. Everyone waits for it to tick over to five, the universal time at which drinking becomes acceptable. CLICK! The minute hand snaps forward and we cheer ecstatically. Drawers are flung open, revealing bottles of wine, vodka, gin and absinthe. Miniatures are produced from jacket pockets, toilet cisterns and potted plants. A disco ball descends from the ceiling. The office photocopier turns into a foam machine. I crack open a Kestrel Super Strength Lager, down it in one, then, with a howl of triumph, crush the can against my forehead. An aide connects their phone to a set of Bluetooth speakers and starts playing Ke$ha's 'TiK ToK'. There is much rejoicing, imbibing and shaking of booties.

An hour or so later, the party is in full flow. Snoop Dogg's 'Gin and Juice' pulses from the speakers. People dance on tables, kicking over Dell monitors and scattering confidential documents. Divested of my suit, I wear a toga fashioned from bedsheets. I have transformed at last from Boris to Bacchus. I am the God of the Party, the Lord of Misrule. I lean against a wall as the room reels around me. I tell some guy wearing a lanyard that he's my best friend and I would do anything for him – anything. I then realise I have no idea who he is.

By midnight, we've switched to moonshine. Revellers are punching each other directly in the face and laughing maniacally. The office has been ransacked, its walls festooned with graffiti and bodily fluids. All the lightbulbs are smashed, so people start fires in wastepaper bins. I am in the warm, dark confines of a supply cupboard, getting hot and heavy with a beguiling blonde. I pash and probe, grunt and groan, wheeze and whisper sweet nothings.

'Darling,' I gasp, 'that feels wonderful. Just promise you won't tell Carrie.' Someone opens the door and I see that I'm attempting congress with a bust of Mrs Thatcher. Emerging from the cupboard, I find special advisers playing Russian Roulette and that game where you stab a knife between your fingers as fast as you can. I am delighted to see them let off such voluminous amounts of steam.

Around 5 a.m., the party ends. I stagger upstairs to bed, while my colleagues pull out sleeping bags and collapse to the floor. A couple of hours of shuteye should do the trick. We need to be well rested to serve our country.

Again, that was all a description of what *didn't* happen.

Everything that went down in Downing Street was within the rules. While gatherings of more than six were banned, the guidelines made an exception for those reasonably necessary for work purposes. Often, activities that seem unrelated to work can be vital to productivity. For instance . . .

Drinking twelve cans of Guinness
This reduces mental inhibition and encourages blue sky thinking. It also grants us deeper understanding of our dear friends in the Republic of Ireland.

Having illicit, office-based nookie
When one achieves orgasm, one's brain produces a variety of hormones and neurochemicals. These include dopamine, which provides motivation and stress relief. My staff needed as many petites morts as possible to deal with the grands morts elsewhere.

Getting in a fist fight and smashing a portrait of Benjamin Disraeli over the other chap's head

Vigorous physical exercise results in adrenalin and endorphins. Both of these promote an enhanced workflow. Unless the guy who got hit ends up with concussion.

As you see, anything can fit through that loophole. If the public interpreted the rules too literally, they have no one to blame but themselves. My only crime was an excessive concern for my employees' wellness. *Quod erat demonstrandum. Ipso facto.* How's that for lawyerly precision? Screw you, Sir Keir!

I obeyed the regulations, but had I flouted them, I would not have been alone. A string of high-profile men were caught with their hands in the Covid cookie jar. As mentioned above, there was Dom Cummings and his Durham odyssey. There was the epidemiologist Neil Ferguson, who merged bubbles with his mistress. Most disgustingly, there was my Tiggerish Health Secretary, Matt Hancock. *The Sun* obtained CCTV footage in which Matt and his married adviser display an idiosyncratic understanding of 'hands, face, space'. This was released online, causing viewers to vomit explosively and gouge their eyes out like Oedipus.

At the risk of triggering the reader, I must note the content of that cursed video. Our hero stands in his office, glancing furtively out the door. He then seals the portal and places his back against it. A second figure appears, one Gina Coladangelo. As hot-blooded as her Italian surname would suggest, she throws herself at the horny health supremo. Mancock responds by palpating her buttocks, her flanks and the small of her back, his bald spot aimed directly at the camera. The couple go on to share a giddy little dance, celebrating their achievements in the field of eroticism.

These images were seared into the minds of a traumatised public, inflicting untold psychic damage. It was like the tape in *The Ring*, except, instead of killing you, it killed your desire to ever have sex again. For my part, I was furious. Not at the hypocrisy, nor the damage dealt to government, but at having to watch Hancock go octopus mode. Above all, I felt for Matt's wife and children. What kind of man would expose his family to such humiliation?

CHAPTER NINETEEN

Ukraine in the Membrane

In which Boris plays the statesman.

The following year, 2022, was a dark time in my premiership. I was dogged by scandal, mistrust and acrimony. I was also dogged by my dog, Dilyn, who kept peeing in aides' handbags and leaving faecal treats on the Number Ten carpet. But there was one bright spot: the Russian invasion of Ukraine.

I'm sure it was a frightful bore for the average Ukrainian. No one wants to wake up to discover Vladimir Putin joyriding a tank through their garden shed. For this Prime Minister, though, it was manna from heaven. Suddenly the news bulletins were full of missiles pulverising cities, rather than what party was thrown when, and who misled which Parliament. With his barbaric aggression, Old Vladdy P had taken some of the heat off yours truly. In my heart of hearts, I felt a measure of gratitude. The plastic-faced hardman was doing me a solid.

This tragedy granted another boon: the chance to emulate

my hero, Sir Winston Churchill. Perhaps the reader is familiar with the term 'cosplay' (a portmanteau of 'costume play'). It denotes a subculture in which nerdy virgins dress up as their favourite characters: Iron Man, a Dalek, Pikachu. In a far more dignified, prime ministerial way, this is what I did with Winston. I rehearsed uplifting speeches, practised making V-signs, even ordered a bowler hat on Amazon. It was only through Carrie's urgent remonstration that I declined to take up cigars. Tonight, Matthew, I'm going to be Winston Churchill!

And wouldn't you know, it worked. Formerly mutinous MPs declared that this was not the time for a change in leadership. Because if you believe your leader is incompetent, you definitely want him in place during World War Three. Alas, like all good things, the Ukraine bump was fleeting. There were countless casualties and millions displaced, but no mushroom clouds or British troops deployed. Inevitably, the story drifted down the news agenda. Midnight came and my Churchillian carriage turned back into a Boris-style pumpkin. Does anyone have worse luck than me? I suppose all those people in Ukraine. But you know what I mean.

Speaking of the Russo-Ukrainian conflict, may I let you in, dear reader, on a little secret? Actually, it's not a little secret – more of a massive, highly classified, earth-shattering secret. No doubt the heads of Britain's intelligence services will be livid at my writing this. Perhaps they are monitoring as I type and frantically arranging for some accident to befall me. Well, yah boo sucks to them: I have a word count to reach.

It was March 2022, a fortnight after Putin's tanks and infantry had begun their incursion. I was in my office at Number Ten, co-ordinating the global response and generally being a legend. The bright red phone on my desk (reserved for high-level shit) started to ring. I scooped up the handset, anticipating the voice of my best friend Volodymyr Zelensky. But the accent I heard was not Ukrainian: it was plummy, English and upper class.

'Prime Minister?' said the voice down the line. 'This is N.'

'N?' I repeated. 'The mysterious spymaster and head of MI6?'

'That's right. I'm afraid I need you at HQ.'

'Sounds serious,' I said, drawing myself up to a full height of six foot four.

'It is serious. And very badass.'

An hour later I sat amid the opulence of N's office, with its mahogany-lined walls and oxblood leather chairs. Before each of us was a tumbler of heavily peated whisky.

'You know,' I said, 'officials usually come to me. I am Prime Minister, after all.'

'True,' N replied. 'But before you were Prime Minister, you were the finest agent in the history of this service.'

I narrowed my eyes, looking unspeakably cool.

'That was a long time ago.'

'And yet I doubt you've lost a step. No, I think Agent 0069 is as sharp as ever. You've certainly stayed in shape,' he said, with an approving glance at my bicep.

'What do you want, N?'

'I want my best agent back for one last mission.'

Anger flared in my eyes. I scowled sexily.

'Damn you, I left the world of espionage behind. It's a young man's game.'

N sighed and slugged his drink.

'Believe me, I wouldn't ask if there were any alternative. A diabolical villain is imperilling world security. We need you to go undercover and eliminate him.'

'Who's the target?'

'Vladimir Putin.'

It was my turn to drink.

'Well, that changes everything. I'm in.'

N allowed himself a smile.

'Excellent. I knew you were the man for the job, 0069.'

I frowned, a thought occurring.

'Won't it be difficult to go undercover? Given I'm, y'know, a world leader?'

N shook his head.

'Our team of MI6 stylists will handle that.'

My hair was dyed black and I was outfitted in a Tom Ford

tuxedo. Soon I found myself aboard a stealth jet hovering over Moscow. I shrugged on a parachute, calling back to the pilot.

'We're at the drop zone.'

With a hiss, the back of the plane opened, revealing the blackness of the Russian night.

'Righto,' I said. 'See you in hell.'

With that, I hurled myself out of the plane, free-falling a while before deploying my 'chute. Seizing the steering toggles, I executed a perfect – and very discreet – landing in the direct centre of Red Square. I hid my parachute in a nearby bin, adjusted my cufflinks and entered the Kremlin.

It is a little-known fact that the Kremlin, official residence of the Russian President, contains a luxurious high-stakes casino. It was there I headed, to meet a contact who could get me close to Putin. I perched at the bar, ordered a martini and waited for the approach. Almost immediately, an elegantly dressed woman sat down beside me. She was a Slavic stunner, with platinum blonde hair and whatever the Cyrillic is for double Ds. I spoke my half of the code phrase:

'Moscow is cold as hell . . . '

' . . . but I'm starting to warm to it', she replied.

I smiled and ordered her a drink.

'So you're Agent Havitov.'

'Ivana,' she said. 'Ivana Havitov. Privet, Boris. You changed your hair.'

The Muscovite minx explained that she was an elite KGB[*] agent and the head of Putin's security detail. However, she had recently begun working with MI6.

'What compelled you to do that?' I asked.

'You did, Prime Minister.'

I raised an eyebrow. She continued: 'I saw you on the news and was filled with uncontrollable lust. I betrayed my country just to meet you. How strange that I should fall for an Englishman named Boris . . . '

I finished my martini and placed the olive between her parted lips.

'My dear, I'm more than willing to Havitov. But first I want Putin put in the ground.'

The rest of the mission proceeded as excitingly as one might imagine. It culminated in a hair-raising scene in a helicopter, a hundred feet above the onion domes of St Basil's Cathedral. I was fighting Putin mano a mano, and had been dominating him with my mastery of martial arts. However, he had gained the upper hand and now held me in a tight half-nelson. He was shirtless, of course, and looked like Dobby the House Elf on steroids.

'You really think you defeat me?' rasped Putin. 'I wrestle Eurasian brown bear each morning before coffee!'

---

* People say the KGB no longer exists and was replaced by the FSB. That's just what they want you to think.

'Leave Boris alone!' cried Ivana. She was a few feet away, tied up and blindfolded. Putin ignored her, placing pressure on my throat.

'Now you die,' he spat. 'You have no more trick up your sleeve.'

'Don't be so sure,' I gasped, tapping my Q Branch-issued cufflink. It fired a paralytic dart directly into Vlad's jugular vein. Almost immediately his grip loosened, allowing me to shove him towards the helicopter's open door.

'Pride cometh before the fall,' I quipped. Then I performed a flying kick that sent him sailing out of the chopper. He plummeted to Earth, clutching at thin air, his face a rage-filled rictus.

'Damn you, Johnsoooooooooooon!'

He landed on one of the crosses atop St Basil's, metal bursting through his naked torso. Mission accomplished, I thought: another bad guy dead. Having instructed the pilot to fly us back to England, I went over to Ivana, untying her and removing her blindfold.

'What happened to Putin?' she asked.

I raised an eyebrow.

'He's now Vlad the Impaled.'

'Oh Boris,' she cried, throwing herself into my waiting arms.

Sticklers might raise objections to this anecdote. For instance, that President Putin, far from having suffered a fatal impalement upon a Russian landmark, is alive and regrettably well.

To which I say, ever heard of lookalikes? I bested the original Vladimir in hand-to-hand combat. Since then the Russians have been using Saddam Hussein-style doubles. Is that really so hard to believe? I'll never understand why people don't give me the benefit of the doubt.

I would be remiss if I did not acknowledge that, at the time of writing, the people of Ukraine face horrors beyond belief. The Russian war machine grinds on, leaving devastation in its wake and rendering the future of millions uncertain. But on the bright side, they get to see loads of Boris!

In return for early support, Zelensky gave me an open invite to Kyiv. Whenever the British were pissed off at their PM, I would jet over there for a photo-op. It was exceptional fun, stomping around a war zone, surrounded by guys in fatigues. My security detail bellyached about the risk, but I paid them no mind. I cherished the experience, visiting Ukraine three times during my premiership. I even travelled there after leaving Downing Street.

Why? Did I need an ego-boost? Was the disgraced leader trying to salvage his reputation? Absolutely not. I had one objective, which was to raise Ukrainian morale. How better to do that than let them take selfies with me?

CHAPTER TWENTY

Feeling the Pincher

Birnam Wood comes to Dunsinane,
in the form of a Deputy Chief Whip.

By July 2022, the Johnson premiership was listing dangerously. It resembled a great, noble battleship, pelted incessantly by the cannonballs of current events. Tory MPs were restive, a gang of lemmings just waiting to stampede. On top of that, my office was leaking worse than a porcupine's condom. I couldn't so much as break wind without Chris Mason receiving realtime updates. Nevertheless, a Vote of No Confidence in me had failed. I was, to paraphrase Elton John, still standing. Then came l'affaire Pincher.

Chris Pincher is a Dickensianly named MP whom I appointed to various government roles. Unfortunately for me, Chris was alleged to have pinched unwilling parties. When the story of his crablike escapades broke, the government denied I knew about the allegations when appointing him. But, of course, I did. In my defence, it seemed too good to be true: a guy called Pincher who acts like he's in a Carry On film? What were the chances? He might as well have been called Sir Handsy Gropesalot.

After months of roiling scandal, my MPs were feeling miffed. They resented being sent out to defend me from charges of wrongdoing, only for it to emerge that I had, in fact, been doing wrong. The Pincher scandal was the straw that broke the camel's back. And also set fire to the camel and made the camel's head explode. All of a sudden, everyone was resigning. First Rishi Sunak and Health Secretary Sajid Javid, in a suspiciously synchronised move. Then a host of second-stringers and non-entities. People who I had never heard of were resigning. Will Quince, anyone? John Glen? Rebecca Pow? The quitters may each have been duds, but the cumulative effect was devastating. Chinese water torture. Death by a thousand paper cuts.

It soon became clear that I would struggle to staff a functioning government. Yes, it's debatable that government was functioning beforehand – you get what I mean. My aides and I huddled at an Excel spreadsheet, moving names around to fill the Cabinet. No sooner had we plugged a gap than word reached us of another resignation. Where would it all end? Chancellor of the Exchequer Jacob Rees-Mogg? Home Secretary Nadine Dorries? How low could we go? Eventually we would have to draft in people from outside Parliament: Ann Widdecombe, Danny Dyer, the Hamburglar. I began to feel like Hitler in his bunker, moving imaginary divisions around the map. Yet I was determined to withhold my surrender.

Allies came to Number Ten, imploring me to go.

'Prime Minister, if you remain in office, it could mean the end of the Conservative Party.'

'Fine,' I shot back. 'It's my party and I'll destroy it if I want to.'

'But what about faith in our institutions? The principles of good governance?'

'I care even less about those than I do the Conservative Party.'

'If you leave now, your legacy is assured. You will be remembered as our greatest PM, potentially the greatest Briton who ever lived. But if not—'

'GET OUT!' I shrieked, hurling a series of nearby objects – paperweight, whisky decanter, darts – and forcing the quislings to flee. I slammed the door behind them and once more I was alone. Completely alone. My shoulders slumped. I hung my head.

Just then a voice rang out, sonorous and wise.

'Boris, you are a brave man. Heroic, even. It is natural that you want to fight on. But sometimes the bravest, most heroic thing you can do is accept reality. It's over.'

I turned to find the source of these words. It was Dilyn the dog, regarding me with soulful eyes, head cocked to one side.

'You're right,' I said. 'I should leave with dignity. Good boy.'

People to whom I have related this story suggest Dilyn did not, in fact, speak. They contend I was hallucinating due to acute stress and sleep deprivation. It is true that the dog had never spoken before, and has not since, but I remain agnostic. Could it not be that a higher power was communicating via the pooch?

In any case, his canine advice clarified my thinking. It was time to go. The jig was finally up.

On the afternoon of 7 July, I emerged from the lacquered black doors of Number Ten to announce my resignation, famously – and stoically – declaring 'them's the breaks'. It was a trademark piece of Johnsonian rhetoric: searingly insightful, pithily hilarious and undergirded by a winning sort of modesty. But it was not the speech I wanted to deliver. Following Dilyn's intervention, I had retreated to my private quarters and poured my passion onto the pages of a Moleskine. When I shared the resulting text with advisers, all of them blanched. They were applying such adjectives as 'incendiary' and 'childish' and demanding a total rewrite. I fervently disagreed, but, between the pace of events and my blinding hangover, was forced to acquiesce. Fortunately, here in my memoirs, I can present at last those original remarks.

Well, well, well. You've gone and done it. You've only gone and ruined everything.

Marcus Junius Brutus. Judas Iscariot. John Wilkes Booth. A loathsome list, to which may now be added the Conservative parliamentary party. Like the aforementioned baddies, they have plunged a dagger into the back of a noble man. If anything, their crime is more abhorrent than those of their predecessors. Caesar was a chap of considerable talents, but he never got Brexit done. Jesus may have healed a leper or two, but he never masterminded a vaccine rollout. And Abraham Lincoln, though a whizz at ending slavery, never once hosted *Have I Got News for You*, let alone crushed it on three separate occasions.

No, the man who may boast of those achievements and more is me, Alexander Boris de Pfeffel Johnson. My Tory colleagues, in their finite wisdom, have opted to defenestrate the leader who, three short years ago, gifted them a majority as stonkingly large as his trouser truncheon. And for what? So they can replace him with Liz Truss, an HR manager performing Thatcher karaoke? Or Rishi Sunak, who can scarcely conceal his eagerness to jump ship to Silicon Valley and never again feign interest in Brenda from Carlisle? As splendid a PM as I was/am, my Cabinet is merely a repository for careerist slugs and swivel-eyed racists. If any of them are put in charge, our poll rating will sink deeper than the Mariana Trench and find itself among those messed-up fish with lightbulbs dangling from their heads.

149

What is the pretext for this reckless act of regicide? Some piddling parties that may or may not have occurred during lockdown. Without wishing to confirm or deny, I will ask the public a simple question: Do you want to punish me for being a legend? For being a leader who identifies when his underlings need a piss-up? If you truly want a fun-sponge PM, feel free to vote for Keir Starmer. That guy could poop a party at a hundred paces.

I am confident my ousting will be acknowledged as an epochal blunder. Borisless Britain is destined to stagger from crisis to crisis. Perhaps Keir Stalin will sentence the unwoke to gender gulags. Perhaps we will be violently coerced back into the EU, with London renamed 'New Brussels'. Or perhaps Just Stop Oil will nuke Buckingham Palace. I expect it will be all of the above. Then the Tory traitors will realise their error and, voices quivering with fear, call out to me for help. And I will look down from my gold-plated blimp and say 'no'.

Ah well, there's no point crying over spilled milk, or, indeed, spoiled country. To my erstwhile MPs, enjoy coming in behind the Monster Raving Loony Party and losing to the SNP in Devon. To the cabal of Bolsheviks that is the UK media, you don't have BoJo to kick around any more. And to the so-called 'Great' British public, I recommend you read Cormac McCarthy's *The Road*, or watch the Mad Max franchise, because that's your future.

So yes, this is Boris Johnson, dropping the mic. I'm outie. Sayonara, suckers. Get bent.

With the benefit of hindsight, I believe this was a fine and statesmanlike speech, far superior to the one we settled on. In fact, if I could change one thing about my premiership, it would be that. Nothing else comes to mind.

Some people said I was the third Prime Minister brought down by Boris Johnson. This is hogwash of the highest order: it was everybody's fault but mine.

Naturally, in the immediate aftermath of my resignation I was distraught. Inconsolable. Cheesed off to the nth degree. I constructed a pillow fort in the Downing Street apartment, and there I spent several dark nights of the soul, stewing over my misfortune and wolfing down tubs of Ben & Jerry's. Nothing Carrie said would coax me out of it. She accused me of acting like our toddler: sulking when I didn't get my way. In response, I held my breath until I passed out. However, little by little, I was able to mend my shattered psyche. I managed this through meditation and prayer, and by studying the works of Marcus Aurelius. Also, I realised I could now earn an obscene amount doing barely any work. Thanks, private sector!

151

At this point, I would like to share a few words on the subject of depression. My hero, Sir Winston Churchill, referred to the condition as 'the black dog', and it has humped the leg of many a great man. Not me, though: I would never go cuckoo. I mean, sure, I'm only human. Sometimes I find myself questioning life choices, suffering from imposter syndrome, plunging into abyssal realms of dark and glittering despair in which one jagged thought could puncture my whole sense of self . . . But that's normal, right?

I'll admit, there are some nights when sleep proves elusive, and I find myself asking painful questions. Am I a fraud and a charlatan? Am I nothing but an overgrown schoolboy, driven by unquenchable need? Am I a selfish sneak, betraying everyone who shows me loyalty? Should I have learned the lessons of *Have I Got News for You* and stuck to a career in light entertainment? Have I made this country a poorer, crasser, crueller place, wasting years of government time amid existential threats? Am I trying to fill the world with Boris because Boris is so empty?

No. No, actually. I'm great.

CHAPTER TWENTY-ONE

The Once and Future World King

Nearly finished.

If – and this is a massive, throbbing 'if' – my time at the top has ended, what will be posterity's verdict? How will future generations view me (assuming they aren't busy fighting over water)? I imagine, and this may shock you, that history will be kind to old Boz. As you may have heard a million times from my flunkies – Nadine, the Moggster et al – I Got The Big Calls Right. And I don't mean the calls to oligarchs, hitting them up for loans. I mean consequential political decisions. To whit:

1. Brexit. Has it delivered any of the things I promised or made anyone's life better? No. But it got done, and I think that merits a pat on the back.

2. Covid. I saw us through the pandemic. Sure, over 200,000 people died – what about the millions who didn't? People should focus on the positives, rather than

unnecessary deaths or the worst economic recovery in the G7.

3. Ukraine. Lest we forget, I was the only politician in the Western world to look at the invasion and say, 'Steady on, Putin, that's a bit much.' Any other Prime Minister would have welcomed it. They would have stood outside Number Ten, toasting with a Moscow mule, saying, 'Nostrovia, comrade – why not roll your tanks down Pall Mall?' BoJo, however, is made of sterner stuff. I stared that Ruskie in his KGB face and told him, 'Back off, Vlad, unless you want a boot up your perestroika.' Just as Churchill gave Hitler the shits, I had them tremblin' in the Kremlin.

Do I have my regrets? Of course I do. I could have been better at explaining why all my actions were justified. I could have cracked a few more jokes, cut loose now and then. And I could have sacked Michael Gove far earlier than I did. But there's no point dwelling on the past, or accurately remembering it. All that matters is that I am the hero of the story. The main character of reality. The cleverest, wittiest, handsomest, most charismatic chap alive. Everything I did was good, by virtue of the fact I did it. I'm sure historians will take that into account.

*

I hope, dear reader, that you have enjoyed this book. I can't imagine you haven't, given how endlessly fascinating I am. Isn't it ludicrous that my original publishers wished to cut all of the foregoing? These chapters were pearls cast before swine, but now I've been able to gather them up and give the reader a pearl necklace.

Perhaps you feel a surge of sympathy for Boris, a political behemoth brought down before his time. Well, you needn't. I am quite content with post-prime ministerial existence. Now I can spend oodles of time with Carrie and our young children. Which is something I love to do. It's not as though I dream of a return to power every second of every day. Nothing could be further from the truth. Nor do I feel like my body is swarming with fire ants whenI see Rishi Sunak on television.

Would I ever return to the fray? For instance, if Sunak gets trounced in 2024 and the Tory Party comes begging? It's not something I've considered at any length. But I suppose, for the sake of the country, I might – just might – agree to be Prime Minister again. It's highly unlikely. But stranger things have happened . . .

Whatever the vicissitudes of fortune, there's one thing I can promise. And unlike my other promises, this is a cast-iron guarantee: I will never, ever go away. As long as I stalk the Earth, you'll be hearing from me. I shall blather away on various topics, telling the same old jokes, doing the Boris act tomorrow and tomorrow and tomorrow. You're welcome, Britain.

Consummatum est.

ACKNOWLEDGEMENTS

Convention dictates that, at this point, I provide a list of friends, family and colleagues without whom this book could not have been written. Moreover, each and every one must be slathered in gloopy praise: 'to my darling wife, for her boundless patience', 'to my editor, Kevin, who read every page a million times', 'to Adrian Chiles, for his invaluable insights', etc.

Well, to hell with convention. There's just one person I want to acknowledge and that is Alexander Boris de Pfeffel Johnson. Big Dog. Me.

Thank you, Boris, for writing this Pulitzer-worthy page-turner, despite your busy schedule of after-dinner speeches.

Thank you, Boris, for gifting historians yet to be born with a scrupulously fair account of your time in office.

And thank you, Boris, for putting up with the ingratitude and small-mindedness of a country that never deserved you.

The fact is, you're the best and brightest boy in the entire universe, and anyone who says otherwise is a jealous minnow.

B is for your bountiful knowledge

O is for your oratorical prowess.

R is for your ripped physique.

I is for your incandescent charm.

S is for your sizeable package.

Love you for ever,

Boris

Update

During the editing of this book, Boris Johnson and Nadine Dorries resigned as MPs. Good news for democracy. Bad news for comedy writers.